Copyright © 2021 by 2 Seas Muslim Marriage

All rights reserved.

Proofreading Services *(editing available)*
Contact*:* aj-editing@outlook.com

For Distribution and Wholesale Copies
Contact: salam@2SeasMuslimMarriage.com

ISBN 978-1-7775795-0-0 *(paperback)*
ISBN 978-1-7775795-1-7 *(e-book)*

MUSLIM MARRIAGE 101

a pro-active guide to creating a peaceful and loving marriage

SHIREEN PATEL

HELPING MUSLIM MARRIAGES FIND PEACE AND DISCOVER REAL LOVE

All Praise is due to Allah. The Lord of all the worlds with whose pleasure all success lies. The One who hears those that call upon him and by His Mercy and Compassion never turns us away. Most Merciful, Most High.

A very special thanks…

To my cherished twin, for *always* having my back and being that voice inside me that said, "you can do it Shir!" and editing (round one was tough!).

To my precious nuggets, whose excitement, love, needs, companionship, and constant encouragement have always lifted me to places I never knew I could go.

And to my dearest husband, for all your help with verifying work within this book. For your faith in my potential and your efforts that I often fail to see.

May Allah accept all the good you do and be well pleased, Ameen!

Forever grateful,
Shireen (Mommy)

Dedicated to my beloved Dad and Mom

for your unconditional love, lessons taught and unwavering support in those lessons left untaught

Table of Contents

Introduction — 1

- Is This Book Right for You? — 2
- Getting Your Mind Right — 3
- What's the Point? — 4
- Keeping it Real — 5

Chapter 1 – Start — 7

- Start Here and Finish Here — 7
- Cultivating a Higher Purpose — 8
- Choose Your Hard — 10
- The Not-So-Secret Formula to Marital Bliss — 10
- Understanding the Nature of Marriage — 13

Chapter 2 – The Journey — 16

- The Journey Begins with You — 16
- Think Deeply — 16
- Developing Self-Awareness — 17
- When We Get in the Way of Our Happiness — 18
- The Brain's Mirror Cells — 19
- In Becoming a Truth-Seeker — 20

Chapter 3 – Being Present — 22

- Being Present in Your Life — 22
- The Gift of Living in the *'Now'* — 22
- Small Acts, Big Consequences — 23
- You Choose — 24

Chapter 4 – Rights — 26

- Getting Rights *Right* — 26
- Responsibilities and Rewards — 28
- Ownership in Marriage? — 29
- The Right to Control? — 30
- Removing Ownership and Embracing Partnership — 31

Chapter 5 – Balance — 34

- Too Much or Too Little? Finding Balance — 34
- Fixing the Problem — 36

Chapter 6 – Understanding Discord — 38

Getting Through Tough Times — 38
When Partners Contract — 39
Unearthing Conflict — 40
The Greatest Lie in Marriage — 41

Chapter 7 – Blaming — 44

The Blame Game — 44
Consider This Perspective — 44
We Aren't Always as Good as We Think — 45

Chapter 8 – Arguing — 47

Arguing to Be Understood — 47
The Root of the Problem — 47
The Layers of Human Experience — 48
You Are on the Same Team — 49
The Angels Will Argue For You — 50
Dignified in Disagreements — 53

Chapter 9 – Behind Anger — 56

Reacting When Hurting — 56
The Not-So-Obvious Signs of Anger — 57
Dealing with Anger — 58

Chapter 10 – Criticizing — 61

Correcting One Another — 61
Appreciation Works Best — 62

Chapter 11 – Control — 64

When Control Crowds — 64
The Leader of the Household — 64
The Root of Control — 65
Boundaries Are Necessary Especially in Marriage — 66
Controlling and Being Controlled Sucks — 67

Chapter 12 – Finances — 70

Money Isn't the Problem — 70

Chapter 13 – Outside Influences — 74

When the Outside World Gets In	74
When In-Laws Don't Respect Boundaries	74
When Friends Fuel Fires	77

Chapter 14 – Communication 79

Learning to Communicate	79
Gender Differences in Communication	80
When Communicating Fails	81
You're Human, Expect to Slip Up	82
Overcommunicating	83
Undercommunicating	84
Miscommunication Happens	87
Guard Your Secrets	88

Chapter 15 – Forgiving 90

Seeking Forgiveness and Saying Sorry	90
Addressing Hurt Feelings	91
Transgression of Rights	92
Why Forgive?	93
What Does 'Forgiving' Look Like?	95

Chapter 16 – Resolution 98

When Stuck in Conflict	98
Reaching Out	99
Re-Establishing Leadership for Resolution	100
When Rights Are All You Have	101
The Honoured Wife	102

Chapter 17 – Happy Marriages 104

When Marriages Thrive	104
How a Healthy System Looks	105

Chapter 18 – Establishing Respect 111

Respect is Loving	111
Is Respect Earned?	112
Boundaries Create Self-Respect	113

Chapter 19 – Intimacy 115

Unraveling the Taboo Topic of Intimate Relations	115

When the Devil's Plan Affects Us	115
Sexuality and Gender	118
Be Mindful of Each Other's Needs	119
Deepening the Connection with Your Wife	122
The Bottom Line	123

Chapter 20 – Love 125

What Is Love?	125
The Universal Show of Love	128
Figuring Out Your Spouse's Love Language(s)	129

Chapter 21 – The Way to a Woman's Heart *(Advice to Men)* 131

Understanding Her Needs	131
Choose to Show Up	133
Neglect Can Be Heartbreaking	134
Support	135
A Word of Caution	136
It's On You	137
Balance	137

Chapter 22 – The Way to a Man's Heart *(Advice to Women)* 139

Understanding His Needs	139
Only After 'Needs' Are There 'Wants'	143
You Are His Protection	144
You Are His Comfort	145
… Just the Way You Are	147
Abusing Your Power	148
Does He Love You?	148
Men Need Space	150

Chapter 23 – Self Care 152

Love You and Be Loved	152
Troubleshooting Self-Care	153
Marital Martyr	153

Chapter 24 – Gratitude 156

Developing an Attitude of Gratitude	156
Choose to Experience the Joys of Life, Not the Reverse	157

Chapter 25 – Putting Polygyny into Perspective 160

The Secular Perspective	160
The Hypocrisy in Polygyny	162
The Mousetrap Men Step In	162
Polygyny Doesn't Reflect A Woman's Value	163
Submitting to the Laws of Allah	164
Polygyny Works When Your Established Marriage Is Healthy	164
The Secret to Polygyny	165

For the Brothers 165

Brothers, Be Careful - Know the Conditions First!	165
It's Not Your Job to Convince Her, It's Your Job to Honour Her	166
It's None of Her Business	168
When Looking for Another Wife	169
When You've Found Her	170
When All Is Said and Done	171
It'll be Hard for You Too!	172

To My Sisters 173

Sisters, It's Okay...	173
No One Can Replace You	175
Is Divorce a Good Option?	175
Considering Being a "2nd Wife"?	177
Co-Wife Code	178

Chapter 26 – Get Calm 181

Centring Your Soul	181
Peaceful Peace	182

Chapter 27 – Protection 185

Shaytaan is in Your Marriage	185

Chapter 28 – Inspiration 189

Introduction

As practicing Muslims, we are pretty much marrying a stranger - they don't know us, and we don't know them, at least not enough to live in sync with one another's habits and needs.

The early years of marriage are when boundaries are set, a person's character is understood, and patterns of behaviour form. For this reason, they are the most difficult years to overcome - *if* they are used to cultivate healthy habits; otherwise, the later years become the worst or most difficult years. In these "later years," negative patterns of communication, methods of addressing conflict, and self-talk eventually fully manifest to create instability in the marriage. Fortunately, the guidance to maneuver through these emotional and mentally trying times is gifted to us through Islamic teachings. We find this advice not in the books on marriage and its laws, but rather in the books on character.

Over the past 20 years, I have intensely consumed every Islamic marriage book I could get my hands on, alongside secular works about the psychology of successful relationships. I have found that in a society dominated by Western concepts, asserted through the use of words such as "new age" or "liberation," we as an Ummah (nation) have failed to see the wisdom in why Muslims do what we do. I have attempted to merge our comprehensive teachings with the findings from secular academics. I have taken from those who have spent their entire careers trying to figure out how to optimize human wellness in all areas that affect our well-being; relationships topping the list!

Thus, this book is written for both husband and wife to contemplate, put into practice, and ultimately, benefit from, in all areas of life – Insha'Allah. Everyone's situation is different; therefore, some discussions in this book will resonate "loud and clear" to you, while other topics might have nothing to do with your present condition. Nonetheless, the end goal is living a balanced life (from an Islamic perspective). When we can achieve balance, we will be able to find peace within ourselves. When we have peace, we have success.

Marriage is a relationship unlike any other, possibly because there are no blood ties, yet the relationship becomes closer than that (ideally). Marriage will pull at our soul in a way that's unlike anything else. It makes-or-breaks us because we often go into it thinking that our spouse is us and we are them. This is simply not true, despite how naturally such narrative fits into our lives.

Our spouse is not us – they are a garment, a cover, a comfort, a protection, a pain-in-the-butt sometimes, and yet again, a comfort. The idea is to complement one another, not to own each other, or worse, compete with one another.

Your spouse's faults are not yours. You cannot change them, and you cannot control them. You can only be there. It's your choice how you want to create your presence in your marriage. Ultimately, it's theirs too.

Is This Book Right for You?

I wrote this book to provide insight into "why things are the way they are" and reconcile contemporary problems with the perfect advice given to us by our beloved Prophet Muhammad, peace and blessings be upon him.

This book will not benefit those who feel they do not have any faults in their marriage because it focuses heavily on self-rectification. If one firmly believes that they are done pouring their heart and soul into their relationship, then I humbly request you consider that maybe you have missed something. It may just be that those efforts weren't what the marriage needed to make things work. In fact, it's likely the opposite. Even if wrong was done to you, there is always a part that you played in those issues. We must be open to that, otherwise we'll fail to see the wisdom in any advice given if we aren't.

I have written this book especially for Muslims in the West; those who desire to come close to Allah and rectify or stabilize their marriage for a higher purpose. It is not an attempt to redefine Islamic rights or to make people feel comfortable. Our religion is the ultimate truth – it is without a doubt perfection. When we can submit to this understanding, we realize every law and every advice given to us will only help us get what we want (the best in this world and the best in the hereafter).

Truth be told, even if we don't understand the teachings within Islam, even if it's hard, we will always find success in it. Allah is our Master and Creator. He alone is the Creator of our complex design, so it is only through His guidance that we will function optimally, Alhamdulilah. Outside of that, we will never find peace and contentment even if we mask it as "success."

The entire hope for this book is to elicit change within – it's not to try and change our spouse. We cannot control anyone except ourselves. However, we can become a better version of ourselves, find peace in that, and witness its effect on those around us.

To create a blissful marriage, we need focused steps and when those efforts are consolidated, it would be considered as "having good character." To achieve this, I have incorporated what I call *"Grow – Learn – Live"* blocks in almost every section. They are practical steps that you can implement (even today!) and start transforming your life by the permission of Allah. With each block, you will access the steppingstones that lead towards the betterment of yourself, your family, your life, and your hereafter – Insha'Allah. The fruits of your efforts can be enjoyed in all areas of your life, especially within the closest relationship to you - your spouse!

Getting Your Mind Right

In enjoying the closeness and love that marriage can offer, there are a few difficult situations you will first have to overcome alone. Yes, alone. Togetherness in marriage only comes after solitary work is put in and not before.

Expect that every good thing, especially one with a reward as great as a fruitful marriage, will require a significant amount of effort and potentially some discomfort. You will be required to acknowledge the role your ego plays and let go of it. You'll need to trust even if you don't feel like trusting. You may need to be the first to forgive or the first one to bring up a difficult subject. You may need to set new boundaries in line with your actual capacity, which might mean you may have to say "no" from time to time. You might even have to start from the basics and acknowledge Islamic rights upon you, and then strive to fulfill them, even if it's hard. For achieving closeness, you will have to become vulnerable, which always opens the potential to experience rejection. Still, it equally opens the doors to experience real intimacy only a marriage can offer.

If you're willing to take the chance, with full knowledge that things won't always work out the way you'd like, you'll be on the journey to creating a more stable version of yourself. While also building a beautiful, healthy, loving marriage (by the facilitation of Allah alone).

Developing a healthy marriage boils down to transforming ourselves into better people and rising in standards of character.

What's the Point?

A big mistake I see with the way many Muslim marriages function is that they work defensively. Meaning, the couple puts in an effort *only* when a "problem" arises in the relationship. Once things appear to be "normal," maintaining those efforts and positive behavioural patterns seem to disappear. So, for the marriage to feel like care, concern and "love" exists someone has to be upset. This becomes the norm in the marriage, only to continue repeating itself until someone finally gets sick of such an exhausting way of living or the couple internally resolves to have separate lives but stay "together."

An argument in support of this mentality is, "why fix it, if it ain't broke?" (men generally gravitate towards this). "Broke" meaning someone has to complain, feel upset, be sad, or show displeasure in the relationship. Broken people are very hard to fix, so why assume you'd be better off waiting until someone finally breaks and think you'd actually be able to fix things?

One might think maneuvering within marriage with an offensive mindset requires more effort than functioning defensively, however, that's not actually the case. Defensive actions (and reactions) do not breed comfort and compassion, they just stall and protect. They are emotionally and mentally draining too. Therefore, one is deluded if they think that when they make an "effort" in attempts to "smooth things over" that they are actually fixing something in their relationship (i.e., only buying flowers for your wife when you know she's mad, or only cooking your husband something special when you know he's upset, etc.). Doing the same actions, such as the examples given, simply for the sake of the other person's well-being (happiness) and not with an ulterior motive, will produce an entirely different result.

In taking an active position in marriage, couples are actively refusing to allow their marriage to be dictated by opposing forces that are constantly attacking them: Shaytaan and his minions, environmental pressures and influences, the jealousy of others, the weakness of ourselves, etc. Instead, they understand that the greatest likelihood of winning the game and achieving those feel-good vibes on a regular basis, is when they are in control of the situation and keep scoring. Such, that the days they're tired and aren't doing their best, their relationship isn't negatively affected since they're already ahead and are winning.

Keeping it Real

The unfortunate reality is that not everyone in the world has good intentions. Some spouses are abusive (both genders are equally guilty of this!), while others can be manipulative and are only there for self-gain. Regardless of how others are, it isn't in your control. However, unless you work to correct your ways, you won't know who's who or what's what, if you're coming or going, or worse, if things are as truthful or as real as you think they are.

Truth is a powerful and scary thing that stays hidden quite far within because it can elicit deep and painful emotions. The greater your desire to draw closer to Allah, as well as develop genuine relationships, the more truthful you will have to be with yourself (and others).

That said, let's be clear here - I don't endorse staying with an abusive partner, a partner that is continuously committing haram (forbidden) acts that affect you or are bringing disease in the home. Or a spouse that continually invites you towards sin and makes it difficult to practice Islam. Instead, it is for us to recognize the truth of our condition in its entirety and move forward from that point on.

As believers, our priority in life is our hereafter (akhirah). Clearing the path towards that means that we need to rectify our condition first, and after that protect our marriage. In doing such a noble act, one must bear in mind that things will become seemingly difficult (possibly even feel unnatural) before they become amazing, Insha'Allah.

We know from our beautiful religion that there is no greater wealth in this world than a righteous companion. Everything awesome and everything that offers amazing rewards will require an extra kick of effort to get to the best of it – marriage is one of those things. Truth be told, sometimes it's an exhausting journey, which undoubtedly takes patience (steadfastness).

The Prophet, peace and blessings be upon him, has said, "The world is but a (quick passing) enjoyment, and the best enjoyment of the world is a pious and virtuous woman."[1]

Disclaimer: While I have your attention, I need to clarify something before some people's defence system kicks in. The thoughts expressed herein are mine and mine alone. Some may agree, some may disagree – that's okay. I have found benefit in it, so maybe someone else might too, Insha'Allah.

---

[1] Riyad Al-Salihin 511 - Hadith 511 - Muslim

Chapter 1 – Start Here and Finish Here

Business gurus are commonly asked, "What can I do to be successful?" The reply many give is the simple answer of "Just start!"

Most of us have our ideals, desires, and visions but fail to start to manifest them through hard work. Perhaps it comes from fear, perhaps it stems from self-doubt, perhaps it is merely hopelessness. Regardless of the reason, if you don't start, you won't achieve what you seek. Period.

> "And that there is not for man except that [good] for which he strives." *(Quran 53:39)*

In embarking on your journey, your intention is paramount to your success. Therefore, "to *start*" is to intend to do a thing and then work towards it (by the facilitation of Allah). Starting doesn't require perfection, but rather it is just as it says: a start, which suggests that you have to refine the process along the way and not before.

Du'aa is an excellent way of establishing our intentions and seeking Allah's help. In the Quran, there is a particular verse that describes the servants of Allah and what they would supplicate.

This supplication transforms marriages!

رَبَّنَا هَبْ لَنَا مِنْ أَزْوَاجِنَا وَذُرِّيَّاتِنَا قُرَّةَ أَعْيُنٍ وَاجْعَلْنَا لِلْمُتَّقِينَ إِمَامًا ﴿٧٤﴾

(Rabbana hab lana min azwajina wa dhurriyatina qurrata a`yunin wa'j`alna li'l muttaqina imama)

> "Our Lord! Bestow on us from our wives and our offspring the comfort of our eyes, and make us leaders of the muttaqun (the pious)." *(Quran 25:74)*

I simply cannot find the words to describe how powerful this du'aa is in your marriage. I don't wish that you "test" it because then it would be as if you're trying to test Allah, a'uthobillah. What I'm asking is that you memorize it and commit to reciting it daily. I am thoroughly convinced that from this du'aa much of the barakah (blessings) in our efforts will come.

In my personal experience, I have found nothing more calming and settling to my heart, especially during times of conflict, than this du'aa. I have found that by reciting this du'aa, my heart is open to doing the necessary work that I would otherwise have dug my heels in and said, "I shouldn't be the one making all the effort!"

By constantly reciting this beautiful du'aa, you are also establishing your intention to create a blissful marriage, one with love and mercy. Also, while reciting this supplication, consider including the intention of establishing a habit of the believers which Allah specifically described, in the hopes to be counted among them one day (Insha'Allah).

It is my belief, through personal experience, that if you read this entire book but fail to implement this "start," then your journey will falter much and feel like an uphill battle – and Allah knows best!

Cultivating a Higher Purpose

There are many reasons people hope to change their marriage, but let your ultimate goal be Allah's pleasure because then you will never feel at a loss. Marriage is a means to great honour in the hereafter, for both husband and wife. Cultivating a deep sense of purpose in one's marriage will keep the relationship secure rather than simply being held together by emotional states. A higher purpose will create an environment that pushes each partner to rise above these ever-changing states for the sake of their ultimate goal - Jannah!

The status of a wife is powerful, but it also comes with a deep emotional struggle. However, let the reward serve as motivation to keep pushing through.

The Messenger of Allah, peace and blessings be upon him, said, "If a woman prays her five prayers, fasts her month of Ramadan, guards her chastity, and obeys her husband, she will enter Paradise from any gate she wishes."[2]

---

[2] Ṣaḥīḥ Ibn Ḥibbān 4252

For a husband, he too can achieve great success through his family. Let such a noble status be his motivation in times of difficulty and mental exhaustion.

The Messenger of Allah, peace and blessings be upon him, said, "The best of you are the best to their families, and I am the best to my family. When your companion dies, then do not abuse him."[3]

If you simply do better for your husband or wife while things are good, you'll be happy to keep going for some time – but when the inevitable words or actions that cut deep come along, you'll start to abandon your efforts. Understanding "why you do what you do" is a great asset in moving forward and staying consistent in your actions. There is no greater motivation than wanting to draw close to Allah and earn His pleasure.

Ultimately, we can only maintain any of our actions if they are beyond ourselves and above "people-pleasing." Keep your eye on the prize (Jannah), and everything gets easier, despite requiring serious work. This life and the nature of the Dunya (worldly affairs) will always be work.

"Indeed We have created man (to live) in hard struggle." *(Quran 90:4)*

The Messenger of Allah, peace and blessings be upon him, said, "Whoever Allah provides with a righteous wife, Allah has assisted him in half of his religion. Let him fear Allah regarding the second half."[4]

If marriage is viewed as an act of worship (as it should be), in which prescribed measures and boundaries dictate how we are to function within this union, then by Allah's permission and acceptance, we will be in a significantly better spiritual state. While this is an ideal way of viewing marriage, it is also the most sustainable perspective, ultimately leading to success – Insha'Allah.

---

[3] Sunan al-Tirmidhi 3895
[4] Al-Mu'jam Al-Awsaṭ 992 - Al-Tabarani

Choose Your Hard

I came across a simple solution to alter one's mindset for overcoming difficulties. This concept is simply articulated as "choose your hard." I think it's brilliant because you will always have challenges and obstacles that you'll need to overcome no matter what you do in life. There are positives and negatives to every situation, but until we keep our feet planted, ready to overcome, we'll continue thinking that the grass is greener on the other side.

By His permission, Allah has given us the choice to do as we wish while on this earth. It is for no one but ourselves to choose goodness, regardless of how hard it is. Unfortunately, sometimes we may say we want to do good, and we may even think we're doing good, but in reality, we aren't. This mental confusion can happen because buried deep within our subconscious are hidden motives (control, status, etc.) masked by untrue narratives, yet we believe it as the ultimate truth.

Through contemplation, each layer is pulled away, our core becomes visible, and we begin to realize many things. It is through these realizations that our life transforms in ways one would have never thought (Insha'Allah).

The Quran beautifully reminds us of the positive nature of marriage:

> "And among His Signs is this, that He created for you wives from among yourselves, that you may find repose in them, and He has put between you affection and mercy. Verily, in that are indeed signs for a people who reflect." *(Quran 30:21)*

So, always try to keep in mind: 1) Allah is in control, and 2) He grants success to those who make an effort.

The Not-So-Secret Formula to Marital Bliss

There are three components to creating a stable, safe, healthy, beautiful, soulmate-tingling marriage: du'aa, the elevation of character, and fulfilling needs.

The first two: du'aa and elevation of character, are very personal. They have little to do with your partner and everything to do with you. Du'aa is your spiritual connection and food for your soul. While elevation of character brings forth the fulfillment of life and nourishment for your heart, as it is where your mental and emotional well-being live. If one does not feel satisfied internally, they will never find contentment in their marriage because one human being, even as close as a spouse, cannot give you that. They can enhance your life, but they are not responsible, nor are they capable of making you fulfilled in it.

The third part comes from fulfilling the needs of your partner, thus directly impacting your marriage. However, without the first two parts properly rooted, this third part becomes very difficult and sometimes even feels impossible.

Here's why each component plays a part in your marriage:

1. Du'aa

We start with du'aa because without Allah's facilitation we will not have the wisdom or strength to even be able to rise in character. It also establishes an understanding that attaining marital bliss, despite making conscious efforts, is ultimately a gift from Allah.

2. Elevation of Character

The Prophet Muhammad, peace and blessings be upon him, enjoyed 25 years with his wife Khadijah, may Allah be pleased with her, in which they disagreed only once. Both were known to have the highest character and both, even without the call of Islam, turned to the Oneness of Allah. They submitted to what was upright and just, regardless of how others in their social circle behaved (I discuss outside influences in later chapters).

An indication of the level of companionship and depth of love the Prophet, peace be upon him, had for his wife Khadijah, may Allah be pleased with her, was that not a day went by after she died that he did not mention her name. It was to such an extent that his wife thereafter, Aisha, may Allah be pleased with her, felt jealous of Khadijah despite never having met her nor her even being alive.

After the death of Khadijah, when her sister Halaa would come to visit the Prophet, peace and blessings be upon him, they would spend hours just talking about Khadijah. Khadijah penetrated his heart and attained perfect faith through her amazing character. Their relationship was a display of great, unconditional support towards one another. Also, they were both committed to the truth - the first requirement necessary in transforming one's character, as truth allows us to recognize our faults first.

Prophet Muhammad, peace and blessings be upon him, said, "It is obligatory for you to tell the truth, for the truth leads to virtue and virtue leads to Paradise, and the man who continues to speak the truth and endeavours to tell the truth is eventually recorded as truthful with Allah, and beware of the telling of a lie for telling of a lie leads to obscenity and obscenity leads to Hellfire, and the person who keeps telling lies and endeavours to tell a lie is recorded as a liar with Allah."[5]

The Prophet, peace and blessing be upon him, also said, "Guarantee for me six things, and I will guarantee Paradise for you: (1) Tell the truth when you speak, (2) and fulfill your promises, (3) and be faithful when you are trusted, (4) and safeguard your private parts, (5) and lower your gaze, (6) and withhold your hands (from harming others)."[6]

The fruit of good character is Paradise, and while it's not easy to do, especially in a society that has lost the notion of integrity, basic courtesy, and manners, it remains the most excellent characteristic of a believer, after tawhid (the Oneness of Allah).

3. Fulfilling Needs

Your spouse's primary, general needs from an Islamic perspective are outlined through the rights we must fulfill and what we are entitled to receive. Of course, these rights specify general needs and do not

---

[5] Sahih Muslim 2607 c - Book 32, Hadith 6309
[6] Ibn Khuzaimah (3/91, Ibn Hibbaan (107) and al-Haakim (4/358-359)

narrow in on individual needs or wants. As such, I discuss this aspect in detail throughout this book.

If we pay better attention, we'll see that our spouses are yelling their needs at us, but since we, too, are caught up in our own emotions and needs, we fail to truly hear what they are saying.

Expressing needs makes us vulnerable, possibly even feel silly; therefore, they are not often expressed clearly or even understood by our own selves. This leads to confusion and a muddle of expectations that leaves the marriage feeling like a losing battle.

Unfortunately, even though it's not exactly spelled out all the time, failing to fulfill a spouse's needs is almost instantly going to cause conflict. Human nature is such that when needs go unfulfilled by the person we are dependent on to fulfill them, it creates deep resentment. Unless rectified, it is also likely the lead cause to an eventual divorce.

If partners become attentive to the core needs of each other, then a lot of unnecessary conflicts can be avoided, and dealing with marital issues would not feel so weighty and emotionally draining.

If you commit to doing these three things (dua'a, elevation of character and fulfilling needs), with sincere intentions, followed by genuine actions (even if you don't always get it right), you'll be steering closer to Allah, Insha'Allah.

Marital bliss is really a solo journey for half of it, while the other half consists of creating mutual respect, compassion, and mercy throughout your relational interactions.

Understanding the Nature of Marriage

Our upbringing plays a huge role in how we understand marriage. Often, this is learned from our parents, grandparents, or any influential source in our childhood. Alongside that, we have outside influences, such as the media, which often creates unrealistic expectations of what marriage offers. Typically, marriage is understood as love and romance, but as a God-fearing Muslim, this is rarely how marriage begins; yet it is very much how it is designed to become.

It's important to approach the subject of marriage with a realistic idea of what it actually is or has the potential to become. To truly understand marriage, we have to start with what it is not. This way, we can differentiate between the subtle nuances presented in relationships, so we can then distinguish which ones belong to the real journey of marriage and which belong to the whisperings of Shaytaan, the evils within ourselves, and our surroundings.

What Marriage is *Not*
- It's not a love obsession that keeps your mind senseless and your heart aching. That's infatuation, which studies show, will likely only last a maximum of two years.
- It's not demanding, and it's not controlling.
- It does not create fear or anxiety.
- It's not perfect (you will forever be working on it, but the longer you're together, the easier it gets).
- It's not the end of freedom; instead, it is a means to check ourselves and become balanced, which is liberating.
- It's not flowers and poetry (these won't make a healthy marriage, but they can add spark to it if done correctly).

What Marriage *Is*
- It's a journey to discovering yourself: strengths, weaknesses, triggers, boundaries, fears, etc.
- It's a means of peace and comfort.
- It's gentle and compromising.
- It's vulnerability and with that, sometimes, heartbreaking.
- It's hard work, but the most rewarding work you'll ever embark on (arguably more than parenting).
- It can be selfless but also selfish, both necessary when applied in balance.
- It's true love when real understanding develops.
- It's sharing but also learning when to withhold, when beyond your capacity.
- It's a means to be honoured in Paradise, but it is also a means to Hell.
- It's a trial, and when one overcomes the bumps along the way, it quickly turns into a mercy.

- It's an unusual relationship because two strangers are enveloped with love and mercy until they choose the opposite of that.
- It's acceptance of what is beyond one's control (i.e., a person's personality and habits).

Developing an understanding of marriage can save many from an avoidable heartbreaking end. There are so many times when two good people marry, but they can't seem to see eye-to-eye. This is not because there is something wrong with one of them (or both) or that they are not compatible. In fact, many times, when couples drift apart, it only takes a few or one right change for the whole situation to turn around. Therefore, eventually creating the peace and comfort we all yearn to have in our marriage.

The bottom line is a happy marriage takes a focused effort to achieve. If you're willing to learn about yourself, your partner, and what is pleasing to Allah, then by His permission, you will nurture a union showered with His love and mercy.

Grow × Learn × Live

Look at the lists above and add to them. Get a good idea of what a marriage is because without understanding it, you'll succumb to despair and feel as though there is no way towards happiness within your marriage. You might even discover that you may also be setting yourself up for failure because your ideals (possibly subconscious) might not even be real.

Chapter 2 – The Journey

The Journey Begins with You

There is more to this world than "the pursuit of happiness," even though society likes to push this concept as the "be all, end all" of life. We are socially accustomed to believe that our present state matters most, despite it being a simplistic, fleeting promise.

As believers, we are directed to more than just seeking these cursory emotional induced states such as happiness, which can quite literally change instantly. Instead, we aspire towards peace within ourselves and contentment in life for what it is. Unfortunately, getting to that warm, fuzzy, good stuff in life, requires one to do a bit of digging.

"Self-awareness" is a word that is thrown around a lot these days. It could even be considered a trend in today's society, one endorsed through activities such as yoga (balance between mind and body), that includes meditation. For a Muslim, it is well established that Islam is grounded in self-reflection, which academics understand as "the ability to see ourselves clearly – who we are, how others see us and how we fit into the world."[7] Our teachings and practices heavily advocate the idea of sakinah (peace of mind or inner peace).

Self-reflective awareness is like an onion. It's full of layers; the deeper you go, the more solid you are and the fewer tears you'll have. This means it isn't necessarily a comfortable journey, and our brains will try to pull us away from anything that might conceivably cause us discomfort.

So, where and how does a Muslim begin this journey?

Think Deeply

The Prophet Muhammad, peace and blessings be upon him, paved the way towards achieving success in this life and the hereafter; all we have to do is follow his lead! Before prophethood, our beloved Prophet, peace and blessings be upon him, used to retreat to the cave

---

[7] Tasha Eurich

of Hira. In complete solitude, he would meditate for days and weeks on end. He did this for three years before tasked with the responsibility of conveying the message of Islam. After the call to prophethood, while everyone slept, he would awaken and pray during the last part of the night – a time that also granted him solitude.

Allah directs us to this fundamental concept of meditation through deep contemplation:

"Then do they not reflect upon the Quran? ..." *(Quran 4:82)*

"Those who remember Allah (always, and in prayers) standing, sitting, and lying down on their sides, and think deeply about the creation of the heavens and the earth, (saying): 'Our Lord! You have not created (all) this without purpose, glory to You! (Exalted be You above all that they associate with You as partners). Give us salvation from the torment of the Fire'." *(Quran 3:191)*

Attaining this special worldly reward of inner peace requires us to think deeply about our condition, purpose, life, and so forth. One can begin this soul-searching endeavour with thoughts surrounding their purpose of creation, Allah's greatness, and Allah's authority over them (us all). After that, one can consider contemplating their strengths, weaknesses, tests, and blessings that Allah has given them to fulfill their purpose and earn His pleasure. They can also reflect on that which is outside of themselves and their impact on those around them.

Through deep-thinking, we are able to open our minds to new perspectives. This new level of understanding and seemingly new knowledge is life changing. We *need* to put thought into our core existence to truly see the "big picture."

Developing Self-Awareness

Studies show that while many of us think we are self-aware, 94% of us aren't. The defining difference is only in one word. It seems that the majority of us approach self-awareness by asking "why?" This, unfortunately, only directs us to "alternative facts" and leads us away from the truth.[8]

It is academically understood that real self-awareness develops by asking "what?" – what can I do to resolve this issue in my marriage? What is it that causes me to feel happy or sad? What does an ideal marriage look like to me? What do I actually want or need? What am I failing to do? What are the rights of my spouse? What rights am I failing to fulfill, and what makes it challenging to do it? What am I doing right, and what isn't working? Etc.

Sadly, issues of insecurity are littered throughout our society. Most of us walk around broken and ashamed for no good reason. Everyone seems to be "sensitive" and quickly offended. With self-reflection, we learn to become compassionate with ourselves first so we can do the same towards others. It teaches us forgiveness to ourselves so we can extend the same to others. It opens our eyes and shows us gratitude to see the good that others do for us, and so much more.

The journey of self-discovery can be harsh and even painful. Our mind is programmed to self-preserve and save us from harm; thus, we often only function from a surface-level perspective. When we force ourselves to dig deep (introspectively) into our insecurities and fears, it can cause us to feel depressed and lack confidence. The key is to continue despite the discomfort until we can see the truth of our situation.

Self-reflection is a habit that should remain constant in our lives. Since our condition is ever-changing, we have to keep asking ourselves the question: "What is most pleasing to my Creator?"

When We Get in the Way of Our Happiness

Unfortunately, because our brains are wired to viciously protect us from any perceived threats, it prevents us from unearthing some ugly truths about ourselves. This natural defence system often jumps in the way of our own desired outcomes. We succumb to these defences as they make us feel comfortable in the moment, but not necessarily in the long run. As such, it stops us from being able to rise above the challenges we face. Unfortunately, this prevents many good couples

---

[8] Tasha Eurich

from overcoming relatively small bumps on the road to a healthy marital union. The opposite of this holds true too.

When people learn to rise above their emotional states through self-reflection, they realize that a good marriage isn't rocket science. It's easier than we think. We just have to be willing to think deeply, even if it makes us a bit uncomfortable.

When we are unable to be self-aware, marriage becomes a wall of defensive, passive-aggressive bickering. Even if you try to resolve pesky issues, you'll still spend the next 20 years going around in circles about the same thing – it's exhausting! The problem often isn't that we aren't trying, it's that we aren't focusing on core issues.

Grasping the entirety of the issues we are facing can be discovered through contemplation. Thus, even if efforts are being made, without taking a moment to reflect, solutions implemented will likely be unstable and short-lived.

As we continue to explore, accept and learn about ourselves, we become more confident, productive, and ultimately, at peace. Also, the more you know your true self and become aware of your actions, your thoughts, the subconscious vibes you give off to others, your presence, and how your role manifests in people's lives, the more you're able to find comfort in the person you're with. This is simply because a happy marriage isn't necessarily about the other person - it's about you.

This needs some explaining...

The Brain's Mirror Cells

Yes, a marriage takes two people to work well, and marriage requires both parties to make an effort. However, marriage is also a mirror of our own self. Our brains consist of mirror cells; therefore, we inherently absorb and mimic the emotions of those around us. This is known as "emotional mirroring." You can alter this mirroring by changing your mental state and consequently affect your spouse.

The Messenger of Allah, peace and blessing be upon him, said: "The believer is a mirror for the believer, and the believer is the brother of the believer. He safeguards his property for him and defends him from behind."[9]

So, in understanding that our spouse will instinctively influence our state of mind simply because of their closeness to us, we should also know that we will affect our spouse in the same way. This is a game-changer!

The power to positively influence our surroundings comes from our ability to better ourselves. That means it doesn't matter what your spouse is doing! If you consistently express compassion, kindness, empathy, etc., despite what the other person does, they too will soon start changing, without even knowing it.

There is no question that doing this will be hard work, but with Allah's help, you will find success in doing good. Ultimately, you'd always be winning if you intend to better yourself, to please Allah, and not to change your spouse.

Keep in mind, the reverse of our mirror cells holds true too. So, learn to be very careful with your negative emotions and behaviours as they can influence your spouse. Eventually, that would turn into a vicious cycle of ugly interactions - definitely something you don't want!

In Becoming a Truth-Seeker

In your quest to "know thyself," keep firm in the truth so that you achieve what you have set out to do.

"Speak the truth even if it's against yourself" is prophetic advice that establishes the foundation of effective self-reflection and rectification. Truth is truth. It can't change. With it, you will always be successful regardless of how it makes you feel in the moment.

> "O you who believe! Stand out firmly for justice, as witnesses to Allah, even though it be against yourselves, or your parents, or your kin, be he rich or poor, Allah is a Better Protector to both (than you). So follow not the lusts (of your hearts), lest you avoid justice; and if you distort your witness or refuse to give it, verily, Allah is Ever Well-Acquainted with what you do." *(Quran 4:135)*

---

[9] Al-Bukhari - Al-Adab Al-Mufrad (no. 239), Abu Dawud (3/1370/no. 4900)

The crux of self-awareness is a commitment to truth, even if it's against yourself. In our quest to find the truth, we need to take some time to stop the mental clatter and think clearly. Space is healthy in a marriage for this very purpose.

When we achieve real self-awareness, the heart stirs, and we'll see our patterns of behaviour change. While this is a good thing, it also has a way of making the people around us uncomfortable. When something happens differently than what they have come to expect, they tend to respond negatively. It's a defensive reaction that stems from fear of the unknown. Human nature is such that we find "comfort" even in negative behavioural patterns because they are known and expected.

Remember, being a better version of yourself takes time, consistency, and the intent to do what is better regardless of how people react to you. Your purpose in life isn't to make others comfortable. Someone, somewhere, will always find fault in what you do — always! Make your intention to use the knowledge you learn about yourself to grow into the submissive servant of Allah we were created to be (Insha'Allah).

Grow × Learn × Live

You'll need silence and time to clear out the cobwebs. How you achieve this depends on your circumstances but make it a priority. Consider asking your spouse for some time and space during the evenings. Maybe leave the children with the grandparents for a few days, wake up for tahajjud (prayer in the last third of the night) when no one else is around, or if nothing is demanding your attention, then perhaps take a mini-vacation to a relative's place where you can have some space, etc. Discuss with your partner, your need to have some space and figure out a way that won't be hurtful to anyone.

Chapter 3 – Being Present

Being Present in Your Life

Your life is yours.

Allah has permitted us to choose what we wish to do. These choices, of course, will always have a consequence - good or bad. With that said, no one is responsible for your happiness except for you.

I must admit, statements like the one above: "no one is responsible for your happiness except for you," used to rub me the wrong way. They can be annoying to hear. This one in particular, didn't make much sense to me because, of course, other people's actions *do* affect us whether we like it or not, right? However, I realized that to understand the depth of this level of self-accountability, we would be mimicking the debate of "the chicken or the egg" – which came first? Is it your behaviour and outlook on life that manifested people's behaviour towards you? Or is it people's behaviour that manifested your negative thoughts?

When we can address the above question, we start to become present in our lives and manifest the ultimate truth. That is, we stand alone before Allah, having been given a choice in what we do, regardless of how hard it is. The actions we take in life are our choices alone.

> "And every one of them will come to Him alone on the Day of Resurrection (without any helper, or protector or defender)." *(Quran 19:95)*

The Gift of Living in the *'Now'*

"Yesterday was history, tomorrow is a mystery, and today is a gift; that is why it is called the present."[10]

Being present in life means we understand our God-given choice, to either be reactive or proactive. The former follows a more

---

[10] Bill Keane (Kung Fu Panda)

instinctive behaviour, one that is in line with our personality. The latter is conscious and signifies that we are aware of ourselves. Living in the "now" tends to suggest that what we do or don't do has no difference in the outcomes of our life. However, living in the "now" means that the only authority we have is within the present. We cannot change the past, and we cannot change the future (even if we like to think we can). So, it's about making the most of the moment, rather than losing out by dwelling on what has already happened or is yet to happen.

Do we still make plans? Yes, we do, but we don't do it with certainty it will happen. We do it knowing we're trying to make good decisions, but it's not always what is best for us and won't necessarily work out that way. Living in the "now" doesn't mean being irresponsible. It means enjoying our present state to the best of our ability. Love the process, and you'll love life.

The perspective we choose to view the world around us will help us decide how to react to the inevitable events that come our way. We can dwell on uncertainties until we make ourselves sick, stagnant, afraid or cynical. Or we could learn from life lessons and move on by positively anticipating what is to come.

Don't let life pass you by, living in the past or fearing the present. Enjoy the good that's right there, right now. In every situation there is always good, all you have to do is look for it!

Small Acts, Big Consequences

We are often quick to discredit seemingly small actions and feel "nothing will change." A simple example of how untrue this thinking is, can be seen in the concept of du'aa (supplication). Du'aa contains a special gift, as it is permitted to overcome decree. The act of making du'aa is a relatively easy action yet so incredibly powerful. With this knowledge, we can understand that even the small things, and arguably, especially the small things, can have a profound effect on our lives.

The Prophet Muhammad, peace and blessing be upon him, said, "No precaution can protect against the decree of Allah. Du'aa is beneficial with regard to what has been decreed and what has not been decreed.

The du'aa meets the calamity that has been decreed and wrestles with it, until the Day of Resurrection."[11]

The Messenger of Allah, peace and blessings be upon him, also said, "Du'aa may be of benefit with regard to what has already happened or what has not yet happened, so adhere to du'aa, O slaves of Allah."[12]

If you don't have the strength to do anything except du'aa, then do just that without dismissing it as insignificant. Never lose hope in Allah, the One who controls hearts, the All-Hearing.

Remember, the other person doesn't have to change for things to get better. You have to change because only you can choose how you perceive what happens around you.

You Choose

It's clear nothing happens without the will of Allah, but it's also clear that Allah has given us full authority in this world to choose our way. You can decide to go towards Him or away. Each test you face is a clear indication of where you actually stand in life (or the intent you truly had). Just as in marriage, you can choose to be on the same side as your partner and work things out, or you can choose to keep hurting, close up and never find good in any of it.

I once summed it up in a poem that said, "A test is only a question mark away from a reward. Will you submit to that which you cannot control? Or will your choice be hard and dramatic turmoil?"

You choose.

Of course, I'm not advocating that abuse or haram (Islamically forbidden) activities are behaviours that somebody should accept, or that one must be expected to continue living with under the advice of simply, "just change your perspective about it" – that's silly. For situations such as abuse, one must utilize professional help specific to the actual issue i.e., domestic abuse, addiction, etc.

The advice herein is for couples who share similar values, despite having opposite personalities. They strive towards good but fail to

---

[11] Al-Tabaraani, 2/800 (33)
[12] Al-Tirmidhi 3548

find that in each other due to some hurt or mistake. We are human. Mistakes happen, but they don't necessarily define one's true self. Therefore, there is hope to get through the situation and still come out feeling loved and protected by the garment of a marital union.

Again, the choice is entirely yours in how you want to live with your spouse.

> *Grow × Learn × Live*
>
> Don't underestimate small changes in yourself. Start with du'aa and a firm intention to choose good actions, regardless of your circumstances.
>
> It's true what they say, "two wrongs don't make a right." Two wrongs are a trap into destructive behavioural patterns. Steer clear and live in the present, despite the hurt of the past and fears of the future.

Chapter 4 – Rights

Getting Rights *Right*

We, as an Ummah, as servants that have chosen to submit to the will of Allah and have declared, *"Indeed, my prayer, my rites of sacrifice, my living and my dying are for Allah, Lord of the worlds" (Quran 6:162)* unequivocally accept that Allah is just. His laws alone dictate our way of thinking. In our submission we accept His wisdom, His fairness, and acknowledge that we stand accountable to Him alone. With that, we as an Ummah need to break away from the ideology of "equal rights," a concept advocated by Western laws through the lens of feminism. This includes the obsession of making marriage "a 50-50 relationship" (seemingly "equal" share of responsibilities). In Islam, men and women equally need to do 100% of what Allah commands them to do, and in that there is fairness, equality, and success.

If each partner commits to fulfilling the rights upon them in the best possible way; without attitude but with care, enthusiasm, kindness, and even playfulness, then beautiful things start to happen. Rights are the foundation of a marriage. They are in place to safeguard the personal welfare of each partner based on our end goal. Both partners need to put 100% into fulfilling these rights. Not only as an obligation but also for the sake of being the best to each other.

Our spouses are given to us as a trust, hence we are commanded, not simply advised, to fulfill the fundamental needs of each other.

> "Indeed, Allah commands you to render trusts to whom they are due and when you judge between people to judge with justice. Excellent is that which Allah instructs you. Indeed, Allah is ever Hearing and Seeing." *(Quran 4:58)*

Obviously, one cannot fulfill this great trust without knowing what those rights are. They are as follows:

Rights of husband (wife must fulfill)	Rights of wife (husband must fulfill)
Serve him in kindness	Dowry
Obey him in that which is not disobedience to Allah	Keep her in kindness and release her in kindness
Does not voluntarily fast while her husband is present except with his permission	Provide her with food, clothing and shelter; without being miserly or extravagant
Guard his wealth and property	Teaches his wife (family) what benefits her and commands her to act on it
No one is to enter his home except with his permission	Divorce her with valid reason
Thankful for his favours and not ungrateful	
BOTH spouses are responsible to fulfill:	
Conditions of the marital contract	
The right of intimacy	
Keeping family secrets	
Inheritance	

*20 Pieces of Advice to My Sister Before Her Marriage, Badr bin Ali Al-Utaybee

Rights are given as a protection and an indication of the minimum effort required. **To give simply what is due creates tolerability. However, to give more than what is due builds harmony. To neglect what is due creates turmoil.**

With that said, a harmonious marriage is not when one uses one's rights over the other, but rather it is when both deeply desire the best for each other. When the discussion of "this is my right" comes up, know the marriage is in a weakened state, as rights need not be asked for.

Memorize these rights because it is the foundation of every Muslim marriage. If neglected the foundation becomes weak, and susceptible to cracks, or may even crumble under the weight of the trials in this world.

Allah's Messenger, may peace and blessings be upon him, is reported as saying: "The most worthy condition which must be fulfilled is that which makes sexual intercourse lawful (i.e., marriage)."[13]

Responsibilities and Rewards

On a subconscious level, most of us limit our marriage to this idea of reward and consequence.

We must internalize that marriage is not simply a reward, but it's a responsibility too. We don't just have "a garment," but we also have to become one. Transforming our perspective to ensure we understand our rights and responsibilities will offer us the gentle mix of love and fear. Love of reward, and fear of not fulfilling the rights that we are accountable before Allah for.

When couples overlook their responsibilities and jump straight into demanding rights and expectations, they look simply at the 'reward' of marriage. They fail in understanding that the "reward" can only truly be received when they equally give back to the marriage. By "equally" I mean when both spouses express the sentiment, "I want to take care of you, and make you happy, please tell me how."

Your beautiful Muslim marriage starts when you realize the "reward" of marriage must meet a criterion of mutuality. Each couple is encouraged to rise in character by willingly and lovingly fulfilling the needs of one another.

While this may sound ideal, it naturally and easily often occurs at the beginning of marriage - better known as the "honeymoon stage." At that time, there is no scorekeeping, no history of errors, no painful moments, just pure well-wishing without any strings attached. So, though this may be ideal, it's achievable and can be sustained when in balance.

The difference between a healthy, beautiful marriage and one that is not, is the amount of effort you put into it. It doesn't come easily, but again, it's not impossible.

---

[13] Sahih Muslim 1418 - Book 8, Hadith 3302

Ownership in Marriage?

Islam instructs us on how to live and maneuver through every aspect of our lives. How we view the people around us and how we treat them are also closely related to our level of faith. Considering that a spouse is very close to us, it's easy to forget their position in our lives (just as we do with our children). We can become negligent in fulfilling their rights because we are confident in their love, forgiveness, and presence. While this is a natural tendency, as mindful believers we have to be diligent in protecting the rights over us.

The way in which we perceive each other is paramount to achieving success. It enables us to be balanced in what we do, not just in marriage, but in all areas of our life. We have to firmly accept that we don't own our spouse, our children, or any of our wealth. Everything is entrusted to us with specific "care instructions" (rights), and without warning, it will be returned back to Allah, the owner of all things.

> "And to Allah belongs the Kingdom of the heavens and the earth. And Allah is powerful over everything." *(Quran 3:189)*

We are all servants of Allah, equally accountable based on the rights and responsibilities we have. While this is seemingly obvious, in marriage this understanding often gets blurred. Spouses address their partners actions as if it is their own self. Of course, we support, love, nurture, and advise to goodness, but we are also all to stand before Allah alone. In understanding the true nature of a spouse's position, we do not violate each other's rights, either by not fulfilling our duties or by asking more than what is within our God-given right.

The idea that we "own" our spouse is also damaging; irrespective of gender, because it leads to very controlling, destructive behaviours that transgress divine rights and responsibilities. The bond of marriage does not entitle us to micromanage someone's time or dictate how they should behave within the confines of Islamic law. When we fail to manifest this understanding, we cease to be balanced. If this imbalance becomes a norm in the marriage, it will create issues that typically fall under the category of "control."

Oftentimes many of us don't even recognize these subtle actions as an issue in ourselves, unless there are known and established controlling behaviours. Possibly, because many of us believe we're entitled to whatever we want when it concerns our spouse.

The Right to Control?

Laura Doyle, author of *The Surrendered Wife,* advises in her book (directed to women) to "relinquish control." She explains that the need to control is steeped in fear, and that digging deep within will help us to realize these fears and focus on ourselves. She also speaks about the "power" behind relinquishing control: letting go creates vulnerability, and with vulnerability a strong, intimate bond is able to form.

Unfortunately, we often mask our controlling behaviours as being very caring or considerate. Therefore, the manifestation of control can come through in subtle, passive ways.

For example, a wife insists her husband wears a suit and tie, though he does not want to nor feels comfortable in it. Despite that is not her right to dictate how he should dress, she pushes the subject believing it's her job to "make him look presentable" out of her deep love and care for him. It becomes an argument of more than just clothes but her perception of him. If he doesn't comply, she'll sulk (emotional blackmail), forcing him to accept her judgments over his comfort if he wants to keep the peace. With feelings of being judged, underappreciated, and unaccepted, he will likely resist this control in other ways. Dr. John Gray, author of *Men Are From Mars, Women Are From Venus,* says, "She thinks her attempts to change him are loving, but he feels controlled, manipulated, rejected, and unloved. He will stubbornly reject her because he feels she is rejecting him."

In the case of a husband, he might go into the kitchen and tell his wife to add this or that, or do it this way or that way. As he keeps trying to control her movements, he will transgress the rights owed to him and her right to kindness. It is not her obligation to cook and clean for him, but in today's society it is accepted as a norm. If amidst her effort to support and care for her husband he constantly criticizes and wants to "teach," she will become less motivated to exert any effort at all. His micromanaging is effectively removing any sense of self-accomplishment and, in some cases, even self-worth. This will breed layers of self-doubt and will eventually lead to resentment, if not contempt.

Both these situations are "quiet" and subtle, yet they transgress rights - this is a form of control. This type of control easily sprouts from the basis that we are entitled to dictate, expect, and demand more than Allah has allowed. It is merely personal preferences that we are imposing upon our spouse, thereby resulting in unnecessary conflict. This conflict can easily be avoided if we stayed within the limits given to us instead of trying to get our own way, at the expense of our spouse's individuality and peace of mind.

This subtle display of control is often hard to pinpoint, but it can quickly affect all areas of marriage. Control is essentially telling another person that they aren't good enough and that you don't trust them to do what needs to be done. Controlling behaviours eventually lead to resentment, so be careful how you choose to show up in your marriage.

It's important to mention that even though the husband is the amir (leader) of the household, it's not within his right to control varying personalities. Rather, his position is to ensure the household functions within Islamic limits, as well as consistently remind the household of Allah through his good manners, decisions, teachings, and speaking of the Oneness of Allah.

Removing Ownership and Embracing Partnership

A blissful Muslim marriage is best described as an intimate relationship between husband and wife: mutual physical and emotional comfort, protection from evils, kind and open communication, and a commitment to pleasing Allah. A satisfying, content marriage is not to be considered a tangible asset. It is not ownership because even if you control your spouse, it doesn't mean you will receive emotional or physical comfort, open communication, or dedication. You can put them in a glass box and "make them yours for life," but you will not be in a beautiful marriage because you cannot control the hearts of people.

Each partner is accountable before Allah to fulfill the rights upon them. However, it comes with a different set of responsibilities and with different roles.

The Prophet Muhammad, peace and blessing be upon him, said, "All of you are guardians and are responsible for your wards. The ruler is a guardian and the man is a guardian of his family; the lady is a guardian and is responsible for her husband's house and his offspring; and so all of you are guardians and are responsible for your wards."[14]

You are two different people with two different upbringings. Your goal is not to become one person but rather to work together within the differing personalities you both bring, to create mutual harmony. Selfishness leads to transgression, therefore being conscious of Allah and asking yourself, "Will Allah be pleased with me?" in each situation will help establish balance and fairness in your relationship.

An obstacle that is present in most marriages happens when our expectations of our spouse are unrealistic and one sided. In demanding expectations, inevitable disappointment happens. With disappointment the "need" to change our spouse and make them meet those expectations flares within. But, since we cannot change anyone, the inevitable disappointment hits us again. Coping with these disappointments often means that couples fall into a looming funk which never really leaves the marriage. It is a vicious cycle that fails to see the positive qualities in one another.

In understanding that marriage functions best when it is a partnership of varying personality traits, ideas, strengths, and weaknesses, we can begin to enjoy the union we're blessed with. It is human nature to be attracted to the people opposite of ourselves yet feel attached to those that are like us. If we can see the positive elements of our differences, we will learn to embrace marriage as a partnership.

By removing the expectation of "What's in it for me?" and realizing that marriage is not a business transaction but rather a partnership to lean on each other and propel one another towards attaining Jannah, the chance of a healthy relationship becomes possible.

---

[14] Sahih Al-Bukhari 5200 - Vol. 7, Book 62, Hadith 128

It takes a conscientious effort from both spouses to see the good in each other. Nonetheless, by Allah's permission and with patience, even if you are only trying to elevate your own self, things will slowly change for the better – and Allah knows best.

Grow × Learn × Live

Grab a paper and figure a few things out:

1. Deep down, do you think your marriage (not partner) is a blessing or a test? Write what you think and why you think that.

2. Based on what you've said above, what do you think your duty is before Allah in regard to your spouse? If marriage is a test, how should you behave to pass this test? If it is a blessing, how should you behave to show gratitude for this gift?

3. What effect do you have on your marriage in how it makes you feel (i.e., do you argue a lot which makes you feel yucky?)? What is the role you play to make it that way?

Write it all down and put it away. Read it again in three days and see how you feel about it. Can your perspective change to better your situation?

Chapter 5 – Balance

Too Much or Too Little? Finding Balance

The Prophet, peace and blessings be upon him, said, "The deeds of anyone of you will not save you (from the (Hell) Fire)." They said, "Even you (will not be saved by your deeds), O Allah's Messenger, on whom be peace?" He said, "No, even I (will not be saved) unless and until Allah bestows His mercy on me. **Therefore, do good deeds properly, sincerely, and moderately,** and worship Allah in the forenoon and in the afternoon and during a part of the night, and always adopt a middle, moderate, regular course whereby you will reach your target (Paradise)."[15]

The irony of human nature (i.e., our desires and ego) is that when our actions go unchecked, we tend to self-sabotage. The very same thing we want, we unknowingly push away. The desire to have or hold onto that thing is so great that it manifests in unhealthy habits. We tend to react from a deep sense of fear or hurt by trying to protect ourselves from experiencing it again. We also tend to become extreme in some of those defensive behaviours (i.e., don't ever express feelings for fear of rejection, unable to make decisions from fear of blame etc.).

Here's an example of how this might look. Let's just say a wife feels very needy towards her husband. She may or may not recognize this "need" or might simply attribute it to her intense love for him. This wife demands that they always do things together. She is constantly texting or calling when he isn't with her. If he goes away and she hasn't heard from him relatively quickly, she immediately starts to panic and thereafter gets very upset without considering his potential reasons. She is always into what he's doing and how he's doing it. She wants everything to be "together." For her, this sounds magnificent, but in reality, it's steeped in fear; a turn-off for her husband. The more she pushes to be together, the more her husband feels smothered and wants to pull away. Her fear of losing her husband's love has morphed into an unhealthy pattern in the

---

[15] Sahih Al-Bukhari 6463 - Book 81, Hadith 52

marriage causing her to lose his affection. Thus, she is positioning herself for self-sabotage (likely unknowingly).
Simply put, it lacks balance.

> "Thus, We have made you a justly balanced community that you will be witnesses over the people and the Messenger will be a witness over you." *(Quran 2:143)*

Ar-Razi comments on this verse: The justly balanced (wasat) in reality is the furthest point between two extremes. There is no doubt that the two poles of excess and extravagance are destructive, so to be moderate in character is to be furthest from them, which is to be just and virtuous.[16]

As Muslims, it's upon us to take the middle path in what we do - moderation based on what the Prophet Muhammad, peace and blessing be upon him, has taught us, not based on modern times. Learning to be balanced in all aspects of life is very difficult. It's a life-long endeavour to continually check and recheck ourselves in an attempt to try to find balance within our circumstances. The best place to start is with our religious practices. After that, everything else will require improving our character (keeping ourselves in check).

With that said, couples who take an honest look at their marriage when it feels like it is in chaos will find a lack of balance hiding somewhere within it. It could be emotional, physical, mental, material, or even spiritual, so finding it isn't always easy, but it's necessary.

How do you know when to look for a lack of balance?

A lack of balance in our lives is excessive accumulative behaviour; too much or too little of something over a period of time. While it does not immediately affect those around us, we may sense the imbalance earlier by way of internal agitation. The people around us will likely only start responding to such imbalance when it goes unchecked for a while and negatively impacts their lives.

When you aren't feeling calm or at ease about something, consider it a sign that your lifestyle isn't in balance. If an overall dissatisfaction

---

[16] Al-Tafsir Al-Kabir 2:143

with your life sets in, then that too is a good indication that it's time to look at toning something down or increasing something.

Knowing that a lack of balance in behaviours, attitudes, and even thoughts is the root of problems will enable you to take account of your actions and set things on a more moderate path (i.e., maybe you're on your phone too much, maybe your spending is too high, maybe you're going out too much, maybe extended family involvement is too much, maybe there's too much entertainment in the home, maybe your service to others is too little, or maybe your family time is too little or too much, maybe you don't show enough gratitude, etc.).

When you can take a good hard look at your habits without making excuses, your perspective of your situation will change. This is empowering because it will give you the practical knowledge required to stabilize your life.

Fixing the Problem

Establishing balance means creating a boundary for that particular situation to sustain any changed behaviour (i.e., no phones after Maghrib prayer, setting a financial budget and sticking to it, writing three things you're grateful for everyday etc.). Going in strong is excellent, but it will also lead to being excessive and will eventually be too much for you (and your family) such that it's likely you won't be able to continue your efforts. Find a compromise and give yourself no other option but to stick to it.

Of course, this advice is not for addictions. When dealing with addictions, there are other factors at play that require specialized, professional help. Qualified counsellors will be able to set you on the path of accountability and give you practical step-by-step instructions to deal with any addictive behaviours.

Regarding Islamic issues, keep in mind that there's no room to compromise what Allah has set as law. We only have right and wrong - halal (permissible) and haram (impermissible), period. As believers, we acknowledge our sins and work to rectify them, but never try to compromise our beliefs in an attempt to "balance" our many wrongs.

Grow × Learn × Live

Take a good look at your situation. Look for emotions such as dread, guilt, or an overall feeling of discomfort. If these emotions are present, consider where balance plays a role in it. Jot down anything that you might think is even slightly too much or too little in your day-to-day life. Once you've written it down, give your list some serious thought.

Start with finding a compromise in the issues you are most ready to accept or already know need to be in check. After that, keep working your way through your list – it's a lifelong practice, so keep at it, Insha'Allah.

Chapter 6 – Understanding Discord

Getting Through Tough Times

Every relationship will experience conflict at some point but at varying levels. It's inevitable and with good reason too! Naturally, we tend to consider conflict as a negative experience, but it's a necessary and healthy component to sound, secure relationships. Negative emotions and experiences are just lessons on how to create positive experiences. Think of discord as a learning curve; at the peak of the curve, things can get heated, but eventually, we learn about each other enough to keep conflict levels at bay.

The idea is not to try to avoid conflict (nor to keep looking for it) because avoidance eventually breeds contempt which is very difficult to resolve. It does us well to learn to accept conflict as a natural and beautiful part of a relationship. It allows us to see our partner's fears and vulnerabilities and then rise to the occasion with love and support.

Of course, conflict can show up in many different ways. The type addressed herein is not meant to address physical abuse or disputes due to addictions. There is no place in a marriage for physical abuse, nor is it an issue of the abused needing to "develop an understanding." It's a matter of the abuser correcting their deeply rooted problems that permits them to harm another person. Verbal and mental abuse is also not healthy (at all) in a relationship. However, sometimes it stems from patterns of behaviour the couple jointly create. Thus, it is much harder to blankly assess.

Understanding a way through conflict requires us to understand how relationships function. According to the book *Couples* by Dr. Barry Dym and Dr. Michael Glenn, every relationship follows a pattern (relationship cycle) that consists of three stages:

1. Expansion and Promise

> This is the loving part of a relationship. It is when our best behaviour, thoughts, and personality comes through concerning ourselves and our perception of our partner. Everything they are and they do is amazing to us, and we to them. We try to rise to

that view through our words and actions. This stage is where we bring out the best in each other and make promises, sometimes even unspoken promises (or expectations).

2. Contraction

It is at this stage that conflict occurs. Disappointment inevitably happens, possibly due to the lack of balance and realism we bring into the marriage. Disappointment may even come from our ideas of what marriage *should* be like or based on what the other person has said about themselves but not manifested. In contraction, we expose the "ugly" side of us and sink into our typical, unhealthy behavioural patterns: negative self-talk, fears expressed through aggression and mean words, stonewalling, silent treatment, etc. It is defensive yet raw, destructive and lacks a balanced perception.

3. Resolution

Here is where compromise and negotiation happen. We become more balanced and expose a mix of the best and the worst of ourselves. It's the calmer, not-perfect self, but one that is now available to compromise and empathize yet is still clear on who we are and what we want.

This entire cycle of stages is continuous in our relationships. We are always in one of these three stages. As knowledge, understanding, and all the necessary components to creating a harmonious relationship are understood, the stage of conflict (contraction) shortens, and we stay longer in the "resolution" or the "expansive" stage, depending on the temperament of the couple.

When Partners Contract

Often, when couples are in conflict, they close up and "contract" in some way. They refuse to open up emotionally, physically, or mentally. They cease to continue giving a part of themselves that makes them feel the most vulnerable.

Vulnerability is essential to creating intimacy in one's relationship but can be scary as we feel unprotected and uncertain of how someone else might perceive us. It requires exposing a part of ourselves that we guard deeply and only open up when we feel safe from criticism, judgement, dismissiveness, or rejection. This is very difficult to do when two people are upset with each other.

Dr. Barry Dym and Dr. Michael Glenn break it down beautifully, "much of distance between partners is established to protect our good self-image and keep out threatening statements, requests, and demands."[17]

When couples do not see eye-to-eye, they often perceive more than just the issue at hand, as discord can be internalized with a deep and personal interpretation. Naturally, the other partner doesn't know this, and the one hurting doesn't want to share their thoughts because it's painful, and they need security for it to come out. This can turn into a vicious cycle, and to end this loop of hurt, someone has to let their guard down first.

There isn't a "bad guy" despite how deeply we feel - rather, we are all broken in various ways. Bearing this in mind can help when we become closed off from our partner as it offers us the ability to realize they are hurting in some way too.

Unearthing Conflict

In the contraction stage of a relationship cycle, couples pull away and slide back into habitual patterns of behaviour, allowing their worst side to take over. I feel this is also when Shaytaan is working his hardest to whisper negative thoughts and keep us in the "victim mindset."

It's in this stage of contraction that divorce happens, and Shaytaan's mission is accomplished. It's important to understand we're fighting a bigger battle than just disappointment and broken promises. There's no doubt that the shayateen (devils) are working against us, trying to cause discord and divorce. Therefore, it becomes an even greater challenge to hang on and seek Allah's help.

---

[17] Dr. Barry Dym and Dr. Michael L. Glenn - *Couples*

The Messenger of Allah, peace and blessings be upon him, said, "Iblis places his throne upon water; he then sends detachments (for creating dissension); the nearer to him in rank are those who are most notorious in creating dissension. One of them comes and says: "I did so and so." And he says: "You have done nothing." Then one amongst them comes and says: "I did not spare so and so until I sowed the seed of discord between a husband and a wife." The Satan goes near him and says: "You have done well." A'mash said: He then embraces him.[18]

This inevitable yucky phase of conflict symbolizes the transgression of those unspoken promises (expectations). These promises are often made in the expansion stage and stem from our cultural and individual narratives. Our idea of what is "right" and "wrong" (outside of Islamic laws) is often derived from family, friends, society (media), and our experiences.

Sometimes broken expectations that contribute to the conflict we experience stems from promises we made with ourselves and are not necessarily mutually created: "I told myself, I'd never marry a woman that can't cook" or "I knew I shouldn't have got married, all men are controlling!"

These are narratives. We believe them as fact and as truth. Add that with the mix of Shaytaan's whisperings, plus possible bad advice, and marriage can turn into a very ugly situation. These narratives are essential for us to question and explore because they determine how we perceive the world around us.

The Greatest Lie in Marriage

Among these narratives are also the tricks the media plays. I believe this one deeply affects many marriages in the West.

Marriage is a vehicle to goodness, which means through it we will find love and comfort. It isn't goodness by itself. We don't just get married, and life fits perfectly into place like every love song and Disney movie. This narrative creates havoc in both Muslim marriages and non-Muslim marriage because it is simply unattainable.

---

[18] Sahih Muslim 2813 b - Book 39, Hadith 6755

Unfortunately, on a subconscious level, we have been programmed to believe that the love projected through movies is "real love" (it started in our early years). As a result, our internal beliefs are skewed. We believe that if our marriage doesn't look like what we grew up seeing via Hollywood, then we are doing it wrong, and if it does, then we're doing it right.

Many times, for us in the West, there is a cultural gap between our parents and us (due to them immigrating and us being raised in two different cultures). We tend to dismiss how their marital life functioned, as "that's not how it should be," and we're convinced our experience through television is real, thus we aspire to manifest it in our lives.

The haram, unmarried love story in movies is Shaytaan beautifying haram (the forbidden). Halal (permissible) is pure, and in purity, love is balanced, subtle, and long-lasting. Therefore, it's crucial we check ourselves and the narratives that consume our thoughts.

There is nothing wrong with desiring romance and nurturing a type of love that you consider loving and fulfilling. However, it requires a mutual effort and consideration of each other's mental and emotional conditions. There's no reason to be feeling miserable in your marriage if it's simply because you're holding onto lies that block you from seeing the immense good in your situation.

If you're an idealist, your mindset can keep you unhappy in your marriage for no good reason. There isn't one way to experience love and enjoy the gift of marriage. What we are programmed to think, likely from movies, is the furthest from achieving tender love and care. However, when we are realistic and fair, we can express our needs and take ownership of our situation.

Grow · Learn · Live

Take a minute and visualize your "perfect marriage." What does a successful marriage look like to you? In this vision, consider human behaviour, responsibility, personality, sickness, your faults, and then re-visualize something that feels good but is fair and real (because you aren't Prince Charming or Cinderella with faultless, empty personalities). Think of the moment your marriage felt "right," felt "safe" - what was it that made it feel that way?

Use this knowledge to formulate a new, conscious perspective of a happy marriage so you don't lose out on a good thing that's right in front of you!

Chapter 7 – Blaming

The Blame Game

A massive chunk of life gets wasted playing the "blame game" – it's unjustly defensive and extremely unproductive. I remember many years back when I was at an Islamic conference in Toronto, strolling through the massive bazaar, a random sister and I started talking at a bookstall. I can't remember what brought us together, but in the first five minutes, we both learned that both of us had gone through a divorce - twice!

She told me, "It's not them, it's you!" I was thinking (but never said it), "What?! She doesn't know anything about my situation." She continued, "I always thought *they* were the problem, but after going to therapy, I realized that it had been me this whole time!" We parted ways with a hug, but she left me with the advice to take a better look at myself and my patterns of behaviour.

Honestly, at that moment, I wasn't buying it. I thought to myself, "Maybe it was her in her relationships, but there is no way I wasn't putting in the work in my marriages." I tried to empathize, rise above, and sacrifice my needs and wants (co-dependency). I even gave up the idea of having expectations. I was a "marital martyr," and it brought about no good for anyone involved – especially me!

Consider This Perspective

Katherine Woodward Thomas, the author of *Calling in the One*, speaks about the feeling of being wronged or putting all the blame on our spouse. Her philosophy advocates that even if we are wronged 97% of the time, we can still reflect on the remaining 3% and take ownership of it. This approach does not validate the wrong done to us, but it restores one's power over their situation.

To avoid playing the blame game, we empower ourselves enough to transform our situation. Your hands are not tied. Even if you complain until you turn blue in the face, it changes nothing for the better. If it does change anything, it'll likely only make you more bitter or sickly.

Blame is known to psychologists as: "the discharge of hurt or anger."

We all have a role to play in every situation that occurs to us. Our part can even be refusing to be abused or harmed in any way. It's up to us to set standards, boundaries or even be willing to leave and get the help needed if the situation brings harm.

It's taken me a long time to figure this out because I couldn't understand that in trying to do everything to be a "be a good wife," I was actually being excessive. I was going beyond what was even wanted or needed and blamed others for it. My actions were not what was best for the relationship as a whole, for myself, or my spouse for that matter. It was easy to blame. I needed to understand that I had to muster up the courage to communicate my needs, set boundaries and standards of expectation. I learned that I was the one holding back despite feeling like I was "giving my all." Blame never fixes any situation; it only gives us an excuse to shift responsibility off of ourselves.

We Aren't Always as Good as We Think

It has been my habit to devour every Islamic marriage book I could get my hands on and try to practice all the tips and advice of "being a good wife." While on the surface that might seem like a good idea, it wasn't. I discovered I was not as sincere as I thought. When I peeled the layers back, I saw that my behaviour was riddled with fears of failure, rejection, and not feeling adequate.

I was trying to control an outcome, and in doing so, it robbed others of the opportunity to feel fulfilled and play an active role in the relationship. It has been a harsh reality, but incredibly liberating, alhamdulillah! The point is, I played a very critical role in the issues within my marriages, and I simply couldn't see it because I masked it by telling myself, "I'm doing my best." We aren't required to do our best with respect to trying to change someone's response to us. We have to do our best to change ourselves and take control of our own emotions and actions.

Finding fault in others is easy, but it never leads to anything worthwhile. Finding flaws in ourselves is scary (and painful), but when it manifests into positive transformation, it's profound. The feeling of the world's weight lifts, the heavy clouds part ways, and the sun shines through!

Grow × Learn × Live

What if blaming the other person was no longer an option - how would you feel? List the things that you blame your spouse for, and then next to each point, write how you might have had a role to play in that situation.

Let those thoughts sit for a while, then come back and write down how you can change your actions. This will help you see what's real in your mind and let go of the false beliefs you've been holding onto (i.e., "if only they did this or that, things would be better").

Chapter 8 – Arguing

Arguing to Be Understood

When you and your spouse start arguing, you cease to communicate in a way that may benefit either of you. Even if you feel like you might be expressing yourself, you aren't, nor are they. Arguing is really saying that somewhere in this issue, one or both of you are hurt. Unfortunately, when that hurt is expressed in a hostile manner, it is often received defensively and unheard, resulting in more hurt.

Arguing can escalate a small issue into something petty and unworthy of the tension it's causing. Typically, the arguing is never about the real, painful problem that makes one (or both) so angry. This is why nothing gets resolved.

Arguing triggers defensive behaviours, which is also why you'll never get to the truth about the matter. A solution is never attainable when two people are triggered because they are unable to reason at that moment as they are in an imbalanced, heightened emotional state.

Simply put, nothing good can come from arguing.

The Root of the Problem

People are triggered or deemed "sensitive" when they begin to remember negative emotional experiences. These experiences may have nothing to do with you, but whatever you just said or did "triggered the trigger" (i.e., set them off). Sometimes these experiences may be directly related to past incidents between the two of you (perhaps caused by needs that were (are) not met and likely never expressed).

One might wonder - why not just say what is actually upsetting rather than getting mad about random, inconsistent things?

There are a few reasons for this. The most obvious is that the actual issue is very emotionally steeped, to the extent that it can even manifest itself physically (rapid heart rate, shaking, disarray, etc.). Problems that trigger a strong, sometimes unreasonable reaction signify how deeply affected a person is. It is to such an extent that it is easier and feels safer for them to focus on other lighter complaints.

Some of us don't directly express our pain points because we believe within ourselves we have resolved whatever is bothering us (i.e., trying to be the bigger person). While these efforts are commendable, it is likely we have not truly found peace in this resolution, as somewhere within it, we are lying to ourselves.

Bickering and argumentation do not necessarily mean incompatibility, but rather, it works as a distraction or to cover disappointments, hurt, feelings of neglect, and so forth. When discussed rationally, disagreements are a valuable way to intimately learn about one another and grow into a strong, healthy union.

The Layers of Human Experience

Consider this example: a husband and wife are arguing because she answered another brother's salam (greeting). She didn't think twice about it and just answered it because she heard it. He feels a level of betrayal, and she can't fathom why he is reacting the way he is. The layers behind this issue started from when they first married. The husband expected his wife to be more attentive to him but often felt neglected by her. He thinks she cares about her friends and family, but when it comes to him, he's like the furniture to her - convenient and nothing else. Essentially, he feels rejected by her. He has never told her this because it's very painful, and he risks being judged by it. Perhaps it is also an emotion he felt from one of his parents. Instead, he attacks her every time she wants to do things without him or speaks to someone because he's deeply hurt. He wants her attention, he wants her love, and to him, all he sees is that she gives it to everyone but him.

Another example, in the case of a wife, is that she gets upset with her husband because he left his midnight snack mess all over the living room. She scowls when he's watching a game or is on his phone, and any request he makes, she does it with pronounced dislike. For this wife, her emotional and physical state is worn down from dealing with young children all day - their every need and every tantrum. She used to feel more accomplished before marriage, whereas now she feels alone and like a failure, unable to cope. She wants help but does not directly ask. Nor does she express her feelings of disappointment with herself to her husband. She fears he'll use it as an excuse to avoid taking accountability, and deep down, she blames him for her situation. She feels alone, with a lack of support, and she is consumed by disappointment, feeling that her marriage isn't a "team" as she saw her parents' marriage. She also resents that when she does have extra time (and energy) to spend together in the evenings and she makes an extra effort to rush the kids to bed, he opts for a late-night, hanging out with his phone or friends. She is emotionally withdrawn from her husband because he neglects their mutual responsibilities, and if he offers a solution, it never involves him changing. She misses him but cannot say it because it leaves her feeling vulnerable and potentially feeling more broken. Instead, she maintains an angry demeanour and picks a fight whenever the opportunity arises (negative attention is better than no attention).

Finding a resolution requires security in the relationship before both can open up and honestly say what's bothering them, without the other person getting defensive. If a relationship lacks this security, even broaching a tense subject with the best intention in mind and a soft, gentle, well-thought-out script will still likely end poorly.

Security in a relationship comes from empathy. Empathy comes from seeing the human side of each other without adding yourself to the mix. We all have our struggles, weaknesses, defensive exteriors, fears, hurts, negative experiences, and so forth. Making sure to be a "garment" to your spouse first will enable you to create security within the relationship, one in which you can talk about issues without triggering each other into their dark side.

Humans are complex creatures, but a bit of patience and compassion can go a long way in opening the doors to a solution and avoiding heated arguments.

You Are on the Same Team

Another side effect of arguing is that it creates sides. It separates you from the understanding that you and your spouse are fighting to get to the same place. Thus, causing you (and them) to feel alone and attacked. It indirectly states that "there is only one right person here, and it's me."

You are entitled to how you feel. No one can stop that, but so are they. Even if the goal isn't to be "right" and is simply to elicit empathy, arguing will not achieve that either. Empathy requires a person to feel secure enough with where they are mentally (even physically) to put themselves in the other person's place.

In a nutshell, while things are intense, remember this is *your* marriage, meaning you've agreed to journey together in life and need to find a way to make things work.

The Angels Will Argue For You

Arguing is our go-to so that we can feel understood. It's our way of saying, "Hey, listen to me!" but a lot of times, it's actually saying, "Hey, listen to me, I'm right, and you're wrong."

We argue to convince another person of our side, not to understand theirs. Argumentation is natural when one feels strongly about their point of view, but it never resolves the issue, especially when both are yelling at each other. It's a matter of pride and no longer has anything to do with the issue at hand.

I spent a great deal of my second marriage arguing. I thought that I was not the argumentative type, but that situation forced me to see a very ugly side of myself. My natural tendency is to become quiet and decide how I feel, but I was constantly feeling triggered and lived in a continuous cycle of anxiety and stress. Thus, I convinced myself if I "defended" my thoughts, shared harsh truths, or argued against any criticism, then maybe things would get better. They never did. Each new incident gave me more ammunition to remember for the next time I had to "make my point" or "defend my position." I held onto everything negative to justify how angry I was and to justify how much I felt wronged. It created absolutely no room for a resolution and quickly turned bitter.

Never once did those arguments end in mutual understanding. It just made me hate who I was becoming and who I was married to.

Dale Carnegie says, "Nine out of ten times, an argument ends with each of the contestants more firmly convinced than ever that he is absolutely right." He goes on to say, "A man convinced against his will, is of the same opinion still."

I made a resolution after I divorced that I won't be that person ever again. No one can make me argue. I choose. No one is responsible for the choices I make except me. Even in a situation where I feel I need to defend myself in some way, I remind myself of this: "Why argue when the angels are arguing for you?"

This thought comes from a beautiful hadith that manifests the protection Allah sends down for us, whether we see it or not. We are not alone, and Allah knows our condition. Even if we're at fault, Allah will make it apparent to us if we remain searching for the truth and reliant on Him. Or if we are innocent, He will defend us and our position in due time, and it will eventually be apparent to the other person without ever having to say a thing!

While the Messenger of Allah, peace and blessings be upon him, was sitting with some of his companions, a man reviled Abu Bakr, may Allah be pleased with him, and insulted him. But Abu Bakr remained silent. He insulted him twice, but Abu Bakr controlled himself. He insulted him thrice and Abu Bakr took revenge on him. Then the Messenger of Allah, peace and blessings be upon him, got up when Abu Bakr took revenge.

Abu Bakr, may Allah be pleased with him, said: "Were you angry with me, Messenger of Allah?"

The Messenger of Allah, peace and blessings be upon him, replied: "An angel came down from Heaven and he was rejecting what he had said to you. When you took revenge, a devil came down. I was not going to sit when the devil came down."[19]

Another great motivation for us to bite our tongues and gently calm our hearts is in remembering this extraordinary promise to the believers who give up arguing:

The Messenger of Allah, peace and blessings be upon him, said, "I guarantee a house on the outskirts of Paradise, a house in the middle of Paradise, and a house in the highest part of Paradise for one who gives up arguing even if he is right, who gives up lying even while joking, and who makes his character excellent."[20]

---

[19] Sunan Abi Dawud 4896 - Book 42, Hadith 4878
[20] Sunan Abi Dawud 4800 - Book 42, Hadith 4782

Regardless if two people do or don't share the same viewpoint, or whether it personally affects them or not, if we do not feel threatened, we can empathize with each other and even compromise our views to make amends. The hard part about this is that it takes patience, and at that moment, we have to resist the urge to be understood and the need to make ourselves heard.

This is best summed up as: "the best way to win an argument is to avoid it!"

Grow × Learn × Live

When your discussion starts to turn into an argument of "You did this! – And you did that!" it means you both need to step away. Neither of you are listening, and it's just creating ammunition for Shaytaan to amplify through his whisperings. It's unproductive and destructive. Literally, stop the conversation and call a TIME OUT (T). Use your hands and form the shape of a 'T' and say, "We're hurting each other. Let's come back in 15 minutes."

Yes, I admit, this can be super weird at first, so, of course, come up with your own creative, loving variation of this.

It doesn't matter how you stop things from heating up, just do it. You'll save each other from many nasty scenarios, and you'll re-establish that the goal is not to hurt one another but to find a solution.

Dignified in Disagreements

Every marriage will go through its fair share of disagreements, this is completely normal and expected.

However, a point of clarification before I continue: disagreeing is not to be mistaken with arguing. Both take opposing views, but arguing is defined as, "to exchange or express diverging or opposite views, typically in a heated or angry way," while disagreeing is simply "to have or express a different opinion."

Of course, in anticipating the inevitable, we must also learn how to deal with each other when our views aren't aligned. Confrontation is something many of us struggle to overcome. The idea of bringing up a tough topic with the potential of it going sour is such a turn-off that we'd rather just "wait it out." Unfortunately, this rarely ever gets us anywhere productive. All we're doing is allowing issues to go unresolved, fester and blow-up into something bigger than it had to be.

So, the question remains: *how do we keep a disagreement from turning into an argument?*

Avoiding arguments (not disagreements) is a mindset issue. If we restrain our negative thoughts, it helps us ease into confrontation and reduce the anxiety that disagreements may cause. Disagreeing in a dignified manner requires awareness more than anything else. With understanding, we learn to control our natural disposition and discuss matters without becoming defensive.

1. Control your emotional state

Embrace disagreements as an opportunity to learn. Instinctively, we become defensive and build walls when we are in a situation that goes against our views and/or beliefs. The perceived threat to our beliefs is misplaced since no one can change what we think or believe to be correct except ourselves. Opening ourselves to various thoughts allows us the opportunity to balance and correct our own opinions or perhaps provides further insights as to why we believe what we do.

2. **Be truthful with yourself**

   Truth is the most powerful way to create ease in life. If we submit to what is right, we will not become offended by it. Committing to truthfulness and accepting the truth, even if it's against ourselves, will allow us to absorb any benefit around us. Also, we can easily, without guilt, dismiss anything that lacks the truth and move on.

3. **Look for common ground**

   Disagreements quickly turn into an argument when people make each other "the enemy." Viewing your partner as a threat simply because they disagree will open the doors for you to start feeding yourself false beliefs: "They don't care about me," "It's only about them," "They don't understand me," "They don't love me," etc. The truth is that you likely agree on 90% of things in life, so there's no reason to blow up at the 10% and make it define your entire relationship. Focus your attention on the positive areas you already agree on and enjoy them! As for the areas which you can't seem to see eye-to-eye; either work on a compromise or agree to disagree cordially. Ultimately, if there's a decision that needs to be made, refer to each partner's rights and wholeheartedly submit to that.

4. **Take some time to think**

   There is no rush to find compromises or solutions right in the moment of a disagreement. Don't worry about adding unnecessary pressure that can often make you feel like you are losing control. Or worse, feel as though you are being manipulated in some way. Allow each other the space to think over what was discussed and give it the respect by considering the varying point of views. This will establish a mutual desire to try and understand the entirety of each other's views, even if you still don't agree.

"We sometimes find ourselves changing our mind without any resistance or heavy emotion, but if we are told we are wrong, we resent the imputation and harden our hearts."[21]

Grow × Learn × Live

If you feel your disagreement is slowly creeping into an argument, then abort mission!

Start to diffuse the situation: tell your spouse, as calmly as possible, "I don't want to start an argument with you. I just want to hear you out and you to hear me. It won't happen like this, so let's just cool off for a bit." Try to offer a hug, soft smile, a rub on the arm, a kiss on the forehead, or even a silly joke to de-escalate the situation further and remind your spouse that you deeply care for them.

Studies have found that de-escalating like this is the key difference between couples who end up living "happily ever after" and those who don't.

---

[21] Dale Carnegie - *How to Win Friends & Influence People*

Chapter 9 – Behind Anger

Reacting When Hurting

Anger is our way of trying to control the situation, sometimes even by making the other person hurt as much as it's hurting us. It's defensive and triggered by the "fight-or-flight" response, but it never gets us anywhere useful.

The Prophet, peace and blessings be upon him, advised, "… 'When you are angry, be silent' twice."[22]

Some of the nastiest things come out of our mouths and through our actions when we are mad (hurt). Discussions erupt into a fierce, loud and desperate exchange to try to "make them understand" or unleash the same hurt we are feeling. Sometimes this anger is expressed through the dismissal of our partner's presence (stonewalling). The truth is that in such situations, we aren't actually trying to understand our spouse, and they aren't trying to understand us, regardless of how we express it. When calm within ceases to exist, so does reason. The exchange of these bouts of anger is actually a reflection of the fears we hold inside.

Behind anger is just fear.

Gary Chapman, the author of *The 5 Love Languages*, says, "People tend to criticize their spouses most loudly in an area where they themselves have the deepest emotional need."

Fear often first manifests as anger; fear of losing the person, fear of being taken advantage, fear of being neglected, fear that our negative self-talk might really be true, fear that our situation will change, fear we may not have the financial security we're used to, or that we might lose emotional security, etc. There are so many emotional layers that almost always our anger has little or nothing at all to do with the issue that had sparked pain within.

---

[22] Al-Adab Al-Mufrad 1320 – Bukhari - Book 57, Hadith 1320

Whether or not we mean what we say or how we react, we cannot ever take back what comes out of our mouth or what we choose to do in that pain. Never. Even when forgiven, a scar will remain, and at some point, partners will have to fight within themselves to dismiss the hurt inflicted and try to make it "untrue" in the relationship.

Umar ibn al-Khattab, may Allah be pleased with him, said, "Do not let your love be a total infatuation. Do not let your anger be destruction." He was asked, "How is that?" He replied, "When you love, you are infatuated like a child. When you hate, you desire destruction for your companion."[23]

The Not-So-Obvious Signs of Anger

So, you don't have anger issues; you're just passionately expressing how you're feeling, right? Not exactly.

Anger doesn't have to look violent to be considered "bad" – it's body language, words, and even how your body is physically reacting. It is helpful to be aware of your own condition and that of your partner, so you can reframe your perspective and quickly de-escalate the situation.

Anger manifests itself in physiological symptoms and can work as a flashing red light for us to realize that we are actually starting to get riled up. Knowing this will help to stop the behaviour (i.e., sit down or lie down) before we get to a point of no return and deep regrets.

Dr. Nay lists physiological changes to look for:

- Heartrate and breathing: increased heart rate or shallow breathing
- Tension: headaches, backaches, jaw discomfort
- Warmth in the face (vasodilation of blood vessels)
- Gastrointestinal: butterflies, acid stomach, discomfort or pain, nausea, irritable bowel
- Senses become more acute

Perhaps the above description isn't you, but maybe it's your partner.

---

[23] Al-Adab Al-Mufrad – 3122 - Bukhari - Book 57, Hadith 1322

Within the moment, it's tough to realize how we're behaving, especially when something deep inside us is triggered. Ownership of one's behaviour is fundamental in the transformation of ourselves and our relationships. However, a supportive partner can only help the situation. Most couples genuinely don't want to hurt each other and don't even realize that their reaction is also deeply hurting their partner.

Dealing with Anger

The Messenger of Allah, peace and blessings be upon him, said, "If one of you is angry while he is standing, let him sit down so his anger will leave him; otherwise, let him lie down."[24]

The author of *Overcoming Anger in Your Relationship: How to Break the Cycle of Arguments, Put-Downs, and Stony Silences*, Dr. Robert Nay, advises the very same thing our beloved Prophet Muhammad, peace and blessing be upon him, did over 1400 years ago. Through clinical studies of cognitive function, he speaks about how sitting is associated with safety and security and diminishes the fight-or-flight response. He says, "By forcing yourself to calm down and relax, you're experiencing your body's parasympathetic response in your body, which activates tranquil functions."

Ibn Umar, may Allah be pleased with him, said: "There is nothing that is swallowed greater with Allah in reward than a slave of Allah who swallows and contains his rancour out of desire for the pleasure of Allah."[25]

If you catch yourself being triggered or notice that you have just triggered your partner, then consider doing the following:

1. Hold Back

Do not react while you are in a triggered state or if your partner is in one. You have to acknowledge within yourself that your anger is

---
[24] Sunan Abi Dawud - 4782
[25] Al-Adab Al-Mufrad 1318 – Bukhari - Book 57, Hadith 1318

not warranted, nor is theirs. Unless it's anger for the sake of Allah, and more often than not, it isn't, and even still, it should not be addressed when you are not in control of yourself.

2. Awareness

Whether it's you, your spouse, or both of you that is triggered, you must keep in the forefront of your mind that there is something else there. The emotional outburst happening is caused by a more in-depth, painful issue that requires compassion. Compassion doesn't excuse anyone for their wrongs, nor does it invalidate your hurt feelings. It's simply pressing the pause button so as to not cause further, unnecessary damage. After that, calmly explain your feelings and thoughts.

3. Kindness

Respond to your partner with kindness. Show empathy towards their state. Remember, you still care for each other even in those moments you both find each other annoying. The truth is you don't want to cause each other pain; you simply want to be heard. If you're true to that intention, it'll be easier to take a look at the bigger picture and to see that continuing any "conversation" when either of you is triggered won't get anyone what they want - which is to be heard.

Grow × Learn × Live

When anger starts getting the best of you or your partner, consider addressing the situation with a little patience, a dash of compassion, and a touch of wisdom. This means stopping any dialogue and offering a physical gesture of comfort, words, even a change in your body language to say "I love you" (a smile, a wink or even a cute, playful pout- if you can manage that). The wisdom to de-escalate and wait a bit until you have calmed down will establish a level of safety within the relationship.

Remember, you are not trying to avoid the discussion, just temporarily putting it on hold until calm is regained. Developing this type of response will take time and seem unnatural at first, but soon it will be expected and save your marriage many soul-sucking confrontational battles.

Chapter 10 – Criticizing

Correcting One Another

There is no doubt that we need one another to help us improve ourselves and become better people – Insha'Allah. Even in the teachings of Islam, we are advised to remind one another.

> *"And remind, for indeed, the reminder benefits the believers."*
> *(Quran 51:55)*

For a "reminder" to be considered advice, and not criticism, a level of respect must be established between both partners. In a marriage, we're so emotionally bonded that it's really hard to separate the emotional connection with the advice given. If the advice is given during a time of conflict, it ceases to be a reminder; rather it works as a means to win an argument, therefore corrupting this beautiful advice.

It's human nature to want to point out faults, which we justify as "correcting wrong." However, while it has its place, this can be very touchy in a marriage. Everything is personal in a marriage, sometimes so personal that a spouse might want to obsessively control the other as it feels as though their spouse is an extension of themself.

Dr. John Gottman created what he calls, "The Four Horseman of the Apocalypse:" criticism, contempt, defensiveness, and stonewalling. These four patterns of behaviour will deteriorate a marriage unlike anything else.

Criticism is an attack on one's character and opens the door to contempt. Contempt is when communication is so salty that not only does it lack any sense of respect, but it's also downright mean. Due to contempt, the other person becomes defensive. In defensiveness it's not simply protecting one's ego, but the person "gets back" by blaming, failing to take any responsibility for situations that arise (normally small things blown out of proportion), and prefers to not only perceive themselves as a victim but to also portray that image to their partner. Lastly, there is stonewalling: commonly done by men (85% of the time), is the behaviour of being very busy, turning away, tuning out the other person, pretty much a building metaphorical wall in front of them. When women do this, things are really bad, as women, typically 80% of the time want to discuss any issues, so the reverse of it is a bad sign.

All this to say, marriage should not be treated as a gateway to freely criticize someone and constantly share unasked opinions.

The advice given by our beloved Prophet, peace and blessings be upon him, sums it up beautifully: "If you find faults with Muslims, you will corrupt them."[26]

Appreciation Works Best

In the very well-known book by Dale Carnegie, *How to Win Friends & Influence People*, he begins his first chapter by discussing how futile criticism is in influencing people's behaviour. He says, "Criticism is dangerous because it wounds a person's precious pride, hurts his sense of importance, and arouses resentment." The author continues by sharing the secret to successfully developing the best in a person: appreciation and encouragement. He quotes William James, "The deepest principle in human nature is the craving to be appreciated." Lastly, he shares an interesting study on why women leave marriages, and it turned out that they left because of a "lack of appreciation."

I share the above because we often overlook the obvious; and it's obvious because, essentially, it's what everyone wants. Everyone wants to feel appreciated, important, and have a place in the life of the person they love – husbands and wives are the closest relation outside of blood ties. It's the creation of a new family, new blood ties, and thus to be nurtured with a deep appreciation.

Dr. John Gray suggests in his book, *Men Are From Mars, Women Are From Venus*, that women tend to criticize more than men. For women, they feel it is the only way they can feel heard or understood. So, he advises, "If you are a woman, I suggest that for the next week practice restraining from giving any unsolicited advice or criticism. The men in your life not only will appreciate it but also will be more attentive and responsive to you. If you are a man, I suggest that for the next week you practice listening whenever a woman speaks, with the sole intention of respectfully understanding what she is going through. Practice biting your tongue whenever you get the urge to

---

[26] Abu Dawud - Riyad Al-Salihin 1571 - Book 17, Hadith 61

offer a solution or change how she is feeling. You will be surprised when you experience how much she appreciates you."

We all have faults, therefore, it's not inconceivable to think that your partner won't recognize it. However, just because we have faults, it does not reduce our entire character or sense of self to those particular shortcomings. If one was to angrily blurt faults out or express them to their partner, it is likely that they will feel reduced to those shortcomings, as though everything they do or have done has no significance to you or your life together. So instead, give them something else to be motivated by, like words of appreciation.

Grow × Learn × Live

Sharing your thoughts of criticism would not help even a bit in your relationship – "you are this" or "you are that." However, what can happen is, "I feel like…" or "I feel lonely when you don't…" etc.

There is a real need to sometimes vent, but it's destructive especially if venting is done by spreading lies about another person and not looking for a resolution or taking ownership for your role in the situation that you're faced with. The best case is to open up a blank e-mail and type all your thoughts there, hit "save draft" and leave it. Come back a few days later and see how you feel about what you've written – you might not feel the same. Then hit "delete draft" and let those raw, dark emotions go with it.

Chapter 11 – Control

When Control Crowds

Issues of control seem to affect the Muslim community a lot. One might assume control is a gender issue and that it's likely men that do all the controlling, but that's actually not true. Both genders have issues with trying to control their partners, regardless of their cultural backgrounds.

Control in a marriage can be terrifying because it often opens the door to abuse: physical, emotional, and mental. It's quiet and has a psychological hold over the other person. At the very least, it can create self-doubt, anxiety, and overall unease. Control manifests by imposing one's opinion on someone when it does not directly concern them or is not within one's sphere of responsibilities.

Control is not to be mistaken for leadership. Leadership holds the characteristics of integrity, accountability, empathy, influence, and positivity – the opposite of control. Leadership requires that the situation is *under* control (not in control). It functions within boundaries, responsibilities, rights, rewards, and even consequences. The goal of good leadership is for the betterment of everyone while consistently providing balance to attain that.

On the other hand, control is cut and dry – "my way or the highway." Control is demanding and has one objective, ultimate self-gain. That self-gain can even look like it's trying to "help" others, but actually one is trying to gain love from someone or even find purpose for themselves in dictating how others should behave. Control does not consider who the right belongs to, and it leads to blaming, criticism, and ultimately negative emotions by all (including the one controlling).

The Leader of the Household

Leadership is a necessary component in marriage. "Too many cooks spoil the broth" is an expression that best sums that up. If there is no concept of a leader or "amir" (leader) in the home, there tends to be chaos and confusion. Children can easily manipulate their parents to fulfill their wants and desires (even if it ruins them). The couple's union itself loses a fundamental characteristic of a healthy marriage - respect.

The foundation of a Muslim marriage is regulated by the rights and obligations placed on us (as previously mentioned), but it's essential to understand that the right to have the final decision is not a form of control. It is more than that…

The Messenger of Allah, peace and blessings be upon him, said, "Surely! Every one of you is a guardian and is responsible for his charges: The Imam (ruler) of the people is a guardian and is responsible for his subjects; a man is the guardian of his family (household) and is responsible for his subjects; a woman is the guardian of her husband's home and of his children and is responsible for them, and the slave of a man is a guardian of his master's property and is responsible for it. Surely, every one of you is a guardian and responsible for his charges."[27]

…It is a God-given responsibility that is subjected to the highest level of accountability possible!

The Root of Control

The need to control is fear-based. Even if it comes off as power hungry, it is riddled with insecurity.

Control stems from core insecurities such as the fear of loss, fear of people's perceptions, fear of failure, fear of abandonment and rejection, etc. In acting upon these deep-rooted emotions that are often masked (to ourselves) as: "I'm just helping…" or "I want to make it easy for you" or "I'm trying to be considerate" or "I'm looking out for everyone" - we are in fact robbing our spouse of their position in the marriage. Of course, you can help your partner, and in doing so, it is not controlling. However, when your "help" becomes criticism under the pretense of advice (unwanted), or it turns into badgering, it ceases to be helpful. It also strips your partner of much-needed praise, respect, and feelings of self-accomplishment.

Each partner has their designated responsibilities, which outlines their role in the relationship. It is there, within that role, that they

---

[27] Sahih Al-Bukhari 7138 - Vol. 9, *Book* 89, Hadith 252

should be free to exercise their own opinions and do things in a way that best suits them (as long as it's halal).

Boundaries Are Necessary Especially in Marriage

Being married doesn't mean we have the right to invade our spouse's sense of self. No one has the right to do that. If they like a certain food, a certain type of clothing within the home or halal dress outside, etc., then that's who they are. It is not out of kindness, love, or anything good when partners mock each other's likes, dislikes, even fears or joys. It serves no purpose, not even as a joke, because for your spouse, that is who they are. These are boundaries that must not be crossed but instead accepted and respected. Be confident in your partner's abilities, and if you aren't, then know that criticizing them won't help them get any better at doing whatever you have a problem with. Taking over won't help either. Just as you're growing, learning, and in need of the opportunities to rise to the occasion, your spouse does too. It may not be what you're used to, but not everything has to be done the same way you've experienced it.

Cooking dinner can look different for everyone, but as long as it's done, it's not your problem. Paying the bills can be done at different times, with different ways to keep track of things, but if they are paid on time with no interest involved, it's not your problem. Each spouse has their role, which establishes boundaries and warrants respect. To respect these boundaries means your opinions are best left unsaid unless sought after or if the situation turns into a problem affecting you (or the family).

So, just say the children are hungry, bills are unpaid, etc. – then what?

In a situation like this, even while you have to deal with the consequences of your spouse's lack of responsibility, criticism isn't the best form of action. Start with letting your spouse know how this affects you; try to do it calmly and lovingly. For most people, that's enough. No one wants conflict in their marriage (if they do, you have bigger issues than control). Resist the urge to step in and take over, especially with the attitude of, "If I want it done right, I'll have to do it myself." You have your own responsibilities, and you simply can't do it all.

A partnership is just that. It's partners working together to achieve mutual goals. The key here is to ensure that you both share the same "goal" – even if it's just dinner because for one, that means dinner at 9 pm while the other might expect it at 7 pm.

Controlling and Being Controlled Sucks

Trying to control your partner will lead to resentment because you are essentially telling them that they are less than you if they don't do as you like: if they don't wear what you want, like what you like, hate what you don't like, etc. It's not fair on them, nor is it loving. Some excuse themselves of this and say, "I'm not saying they have to change, I'm just sharing my opinion" – if no one asks your opinion then the implication is that you are imposing your views on them. Don't be surprised when people don't feel "safe" around you by choosing not to share thoughts and ideas with you. If you want to deny being controlling, look at the effects: lack of respect, distance, contempt, and overall displeasure.

A healthy relationship will automatically evoke a desire to please each other. When a relationship is secure, spouses will naturally consult each other and be interested in each other's opinions. It is where love and respect live. If you, as a couple, bypass the work of creating a secure marriage and go straight into trying to control and into making each other want to take your own opinions, then know that you will not achieve love or respect in your marriage.

How do you deal with a controlling spouse?

Unfortunately, it's tough for us to recognize when we are controlling because most of us don't call it control in our minds: we call it "help," "advice," "teaching," "support," "being responsible," and so on. If you are on the receiving end of this behaviour, informing your spouse will trigger them because they likely don't see themselves that way. They probably think that it is within their rights to say as they feel and that not freely expressing what they think is a transgression of their right to freedom of opinions (or to be oneself).

The best way to approach a controlling spouse is to find the root of their fear. Perhaps they want to "help" because they fear losing your company or think you'll replace them if they aren't showing up in your life with something to offer. Perhaps they fear being judged by others and want you to do things a certain way, so others don't say anything. There are several possibilities, but the underlying cause tends to be rooted in fear. Find out what they are afraid of and reassure them. This way, you can gently distract them from your personal space and request that their presence remains positive.

Consider saying something like, "I feel like you might think I won't do x-y-z maybe because I let you down before, but I need your positive reinforcement by allowing me to do things in a way that's comfortable for me. I'm finding it emotionally and mentally hard the way things are right now with (insert their criticisms of you that's causing you to push back)."

Many times, controlling behaviour manifests in the form of nagging – "do this, do that, did you…" etc. This, too, is very harmful to a relationship and is still a form of control, even if it is to get a specific thing done. One would rather not have to keep "reminding," and the recipient would rather not have to hear all the "reminders" either.

Therefore, consider this: if your spouse tends to "forget" or not be mindful of their responsibilities, they likely have come to expect that you'll remind them (or nag them about it later). This allows them to shift the blame onto you, and it enables them not to take responsibility since you have taken control of the situation. So next time there's something that needs to get done, use a "reminder note." Write it down on a piece of paper and stick it on the wall (i.e., "Reminder: Remove grass bags from patio"). Thereafter, don't say a word.

You are not your spouse's parent, and I'm sure you don't want to be. By going into "control mode," you end up putting yourself in that role. Show your spouse respect by only reminding and not demanding, controlling, or scolding – it's not your right. Let them deal with the consequences if there are any, and if for whatever reason the consequences trickle back down to you, kindly ask again. Next time, they'll be more diligent (hopefully!).

It takes time to reform and correct our patterns of behaviour, so be patient with yourself or your partner. Of course, you can't change your partner, but if you're the one being controlling, you can learn to acknowledge this behaviour, address fears and step back. If you find your spouse is overwhelming you with their fears, then learn to approach them with "kid gloves" in kindness and try to address the root of their concerns (their fears).

Grow × Learn × Live

Take a good, hard look at the way you and your spouse interact. One can only change themselves, so I encourage you to be mindful of any controlling behaviours you might have and assess the root of them. You'll be surprised how liberating it feels to let go of those fears and move through your marriage with ease.

Chapter 12 – Finances
Money Isn't the Problem

Finances can create a lot of turmoil in a marriage. Though some interpret their financial issues to be about money itself, there are many other factors that are involved when it comes to money. Money is an emotional trigger as it represents many things in our lives: security and opportunity being the two greatest influences.

With the flow of money in our lives, we are secure in the fact that we can afford a roof over our heads, but not just any roof, one that allows us to feel comfortable and safe. It allows us to buy food at our leisure, without the threat of hunger or even the need to control one's desire in relation to the food we eat. Lastly, it affords us opportunities to go where we want, buy what we want, school our children where and how we want, etc.

Without money, for many, especially those living in a consumerist society, a home can feel severely restricted. Even if there is money, without mutually agreeing on how to use money (i.e., towards mutual goals), tension and stress will exponentially increase in the home. This is because the money available is not being used to take care of innate needs or fears. The fear of poverty, loss of assets, loss of opportunities because of misspending, or feelings of deprivation are all very strong triggers regarding finances.

The opinions of today's world in respect to which partner is expected to be responsible for bringing in money or even having the final say regarding large purchases has drastically shifted. There is a 50/50 understanding of money; "I bring in half of the money or a significant part of the money, so I should have half the say." Logically that makes sense, Islamically this fails to be balanced.

The argument of women working as their husbands do within a Muslim household is largely influenced by the need or allure of a double income. For some, two incomes are necessary to afford them the ability to live in a manner that suffices their needs. Both husband and wife agree that it is necessary for both to work so they can live in a way they both choose, or maybe only how only one chooses.

Islamically speaking, if a woman chooses to work and spend her money on her family, despite her husband providing for her basic needs in the manner in which she is used to, then understand it's a choice *she* makes. Her rights in such case were not neglected, but a compromise was made to accommodate the wants and financial goals of the family. So, now with two incomes being used on the family, the question remains, "Whose right is it to have control over the finances?"

Women believe that because they willingly contribute to the household then they should have equal control of all the money coming in the home. Here's what happens though: a man, by his nature, has the instinctive need to provide (or at least feel like he is the one to provide). A woman instinctively wants to feel taken care of, not controlled, but also not having to deal with the pressure of ensuring her family's safety and security (food, shelter, and clothing). When this balance is taken away, couples find themselves in conflict.

A man no longer feels he has a purpose in his home, nor does he feel fulfilled or satisfied with himself as a man (even if he accepts it and it takes the pressure off of him).

A woman no longer feels she can count on someone, or trust that she'll have her needs met, and it places a heavy burden on her that she doesn't actually want (even if she can handle it).

The solution? Find balance.

Start from where rights begin and continue from there. Where you cannot find a compromise, defer the decision to the husband because ultimately it is his exclusive responsibility to provide for his family. A woman that chooses to use her wealth to help her husband must understand that she does that willingly and it must not come with the condition of control (or having things her way).

Some women argue that they are better at handling money than their husbands. If the two of you mutually decide on who should handle the finances, without putting anyone down or disrespecting each other's positions, then so be it. The point is that neither one of you should feel as though you are stripped of your needs. If that happens, you start harbouring resentment which will eventually turn into contempt since finances have a very strong grip on how people perceive themselves. Thus, while this conversation may appear to be a black and white topic, seemingly steeped in logic, in actuality, it is very emotionally driven and is extremely hard to overcome.

Remember, our provision is written for us. We will not get more than what is written for us, nor less. Allah is the best of providers. We are simply obligated to make an effort without sacrificing any part of our faith, and while being very careful not to be wasteful in what we have been given.

The Prophet Muhammad, peace and blessings be upon him, said, "Be mindful of Allah and He will protect you. Be mindful of Allah and you will find Him before you. If you ask, ask from Allah. If you seek help, seek help from Allah. Know that if the nations gather together to benefit you, they will not benefit you unless Allah has decreed it for you. And if the nations gather together to harm you, they will not harm you unless Allah has decreed it for you. The pens have been lifted and the pages have dried."[28]

Blessings or barakah are something that cannot be foreseen or calculated. They come from conviction, steadfastness, patience, and gratitude. In order to have barakah in our lives we need to submit to Allah's laws and be careful with how we spend what we are given. Being diligent in contemplating the favours we have and taking care of what we are blessed with i.e., not wasting food, electricity, clothing etc. Also, praising Allah (alhamdulilah) will increase what we have in ways we can never imagine.

So, if you are one of those people that feel on edge with respect to finances, then turn to Allah. It is only a trap of Shaytaan to make you fear poverty or loss of wealth. Even if this were to happen, it is by divine decree and no amount of worrying or fighting will stop it.

---

[28] Al-Tirmidhi

Grow × Learn × Live

Don't be afraid to tackle the situation of finances, as touchy as the subject may be. Sit down and clear the air.

Remember, your starting point is based on the rights and responsibilities that Islam sets. Thereafter, with mutual agreement and flexibility, you can decide how to proceed with finances. In areas you cannot find a mutually satisfying compromise (i.e., where everyone is happy), then again, go back to Islamic rights and use that to determine a just solution. Submission to Allah's way is the ultimate success.

GET HELP: For couples that find that their finances are a source of conflict in their marriage and aren't sure how to proceed, I suggest seeking some professional help. This topic is so closely related to one's emotional and mental state, often layered with past experiences. It's important to have a mediator in order to find balance through an Islamic lens.

Consider visiting IslamicFinanceGuru.com for some tips and help.

Chapter 13 – Outside Influences

When the Outside World Gets In

Not all marriages have problems because of issues between husband and wife. Sometimes serious issues in the marriage actually stem from people outside of it, causing strain and tension with their opinions, comments, slander, etc. While all marriages deal with some level of influence, each individual's personality and the type of influences will determine how much it affects the marriage.

Two large influences are in-laws and friends. Both seemingly mean well (for the most part), but for some couples, these influences can be very toxic to their marriage.

When In-Laws Don't Respect Boundaries

In-laws tend to have a bad reputation in some cultures for creating a lot of discord in a marriage. Typically, you can trace these issues back to their inability to respect the couple as their own family and the boundaries within their marriage. Unfortunately, sometimes this crosses the line and leads to oppressive and abusive behaviour.

Within some cultures, there is a non-Islamic view that the woman entering the family becomes their "worker." Her job is to serve her husband and in-laws. It is well known that in-laws of this mindset like to use emotional blackmail to trigger their son into an aggressive (even physical) response towards his wife, using words like "duty" or "shame" when in reality it is nothing but their selfishness.

In the case of the man, some in-laws, especially in today's society, want to assert their domination over him through material "help." This way, they control where their daughter and grandchildren will live. They also feel entitled to voice their opinions on what house, car, job, schools, etc. the couple should have or do. If they don't comply, they are slandered and talked badly about. They complain to their daughter, and she is affected by their unhappiness. She will take her husband to task about their "lack of" based on the opinions of her family, thereby covertly stripping the man of his role over his family.

Regardless of how exactly some in-laws exert their dominance, many times it is still oppressive and unjust. The problem within the marriage arises when each partner is caught between their spouse and their parents. What a difficult a situation, and how unfair to have to "choose sides," yet, ultimately, that's the only way going forward.

So, how do we move forward when we don't want to hurt our parents or our spouse?

Taking everything back to the principles of religion, we have to establish two key points. For a man, his Jannah is with his parents, and for a woman, her Jannah is with her husband. This at the forefront, each partner should strive to achieve this reward to the best of their ability, while ensuring two other Islamic principles remain intact: respect and justice.

A man's role is to protect his wife, which means if his parents are oppressive, unjust, and wrong in doing what they choose to do, it is his obligation to defend her. A woman is a pillar for her husband, she preserves his dignity. So, if her family is trying to lower his state by belittling him, slandering him, trying to override his decisions and take over his God-given responsibilities, then she must stand up for him. This is justice.

Allah's messenger, peace and blessings be upon him, said: "Let him be humbled, let him be humbled." It was said: "Allah's Messenger, who is he?" He said, "He who finds his parents in old age, either one or both of them, and does not enter Paradise."[29]

As for respect, it comes from how you choose to support each other's rights in front of your respective parents. Remember, parents can't actually control you; you're two grown individuals. Firstly, establish respect between the two of you. Voice your concerns, voice your support for one another and be just in that. After that, if your parents choose to voice their opinions, refrain from arguing with them, or trying to "make them understand." Defend your partner with a level head and in a respectful tone. Otherwise, let them say what they want, and don't bring that into your marriage. That's their opinion; it's not yours. I'm not saying we dismiss the opinions of our parents - not at all! Their wisdom, experience, and blessings are vital

---

[29] Sahih Muslim 2551b - Book 45, Hadith 11

to our success. However, when the situation becomes unjust and oppressive, we have to deal with it differently.

Dealing with our parents is a deeply emotional and triggering situation. Of course, we never want to hurt them, yet they may still be offended by some of the choices we make. It's up to us to keep making du'aa for our parents, as well as trying our utmost to honour them through good actions and kindness. This doesn't mean we have to respond to all their opinions, especially where we feel it would not be suitable for our families or safeguard their deen (faith).

Parents are human too; they have their own triggers, their own faults, and their own fears, but with that said, they also have the right to be respected regardless of their own weaknesses. To love your spouse is to show kindness and care to their parents, even if they aren't good to you. Allah is aware of all things.

There is a flip side to this...

Some people oppress their in-laws and see them as a threat to their spouse's love. While this logically makes no sense, people do it. They belittle, lie, threaten, and even display aggressive behaviours (both male and females!) towards their in-laws. Some feel their in-laws are a burden. Others see weakness in them and relish the opportunity to dominate them, while others are simply foolish. There is no place for this. Even if parents can be difficult at times, no spouse ever has the right to harm their in-laws, ever! Your in-laws become like your own parents, as they become mahram (unlawful for marriage) to you. This bonds you to them for life, no matter what may happen within the marriage.

> "Your Lord has decreed that you worship none but Him, and do good to parents. If any one of them or both of them reach old age, do not say to them: uff (a word or expression of anger or contempt) and do not scold them, and address them with respectful words." *(Quran 17:23)*

The Prophet, peace and blessings be upon him, said, "The best of deeds or deed is the (observance of) prayer at its proper time and kindness to parents."[30]

When Friends Fuel Fires

The Prophet, peace and blessings be upon him, said "A man follows the religion of his friend; so each one should consider whom he makes his friend."[31]

Sometimes, problems in a marriage arise from the influence of our social circle and the friendships we keep. Allowing people into our private lives can be a tricky matter because they may not have the same end goals as us. Or they may not actually want us to succeed. Sometimes, the problem isn't even that our friends aren't giving beneficial advice, but it could be unsolicited advice, comments, and general opinions of what a marriage "should" or "shouldn't" be like.

These subtleties slowly compound within us and amount to unnecessary issues in one's marriage because they create self-doubt.

Friends can also unwittingly impose their own narratives of marriage into our marriage, which can also cause issues that, as a couple, don't actually exist.

If you recall, in the beginning chapters, I had discussed the need to establish truth within your life as it allows us to see things with clarity, Insha'Allah. When dealing with others, that understanding of truth is your best friend. It is human nature to want to convince people of our opinions and some do this thinking it's in our best interest even when it isn't. Being truthful with yourself will allow doubts to sit on the sidelines and maintain balance in our life.

The role of "friends" in your life is to add comfort, happiness, joy, and other positive emotions. If they aren't doing that, then they aren't "friends." It's toxic, and toxic behaviour can be very damaging to your mental state.

A general rule of thumb that will help your marriage in respect to your friends is pretty simple: your spouse takes priority.

---

[30] Sahih Muslim 85e - Book 1, Hadith 162
[31] Sunan Abi Dawud 4833 - Book 43, Hadith 61

If you're the type to put your friends' needs over your spouse, know that this will lead to many problems over time. If you're neglecting your family so you can play the hero to your friends, then expect over time, your spouse will feel slighted, neglected, and even resentful. They may start making side remarks about your friends or even their place in your life.

The priority, including opinions and how you as a couple should lead your life, should always be given to your spouse. After all, you're a team, working together to make in this life and the hereafter, Insha'Allah.

Your marital relationship continuously needs to be put first, securing it through finding mutual compromises based on your personal needs and wants and not those of your outside circle.

Even with friends, there is more to consider…

Spouses can neglect one another by being "busy" all the time and not making time for each other. For some people, quality time means a lot to them, and if they've repeatedly attempted to seek that from their spouse with no avail, then it's expected they'll go looking elsewhere. If having someone to talk to, spend time with, and offer companionship is not mutually developed in the relationship, then, of course, people will be inclined to find that through friendships, possibly even in an excessive manner.

Spouses that complain that their partner puts their friends above them should consider taking an honest look at how they "show up" and their role in the marriage (it's likely a mutual complaint). If they aren't around much, how can one expect their spouse to keep waiting for them to want to offer their companionship?

Making each other a priority has to be mutual, otherwise it won't hold.

Chapter 14 – Communication

Learning to Communicate

When learning to communicate, your tone of voice and body language matter more than the words that come out of your mouth. There are many struggling relationships because couples don't take responsibility for more than their words (sometimes, not even that). Often, the onset of discord isn't even about what was "said" but about how thoughts and emotions were expressed. These behaviours become a pattern in how we communicate with one another, and each negative interaction will work to chip at the foundation of the relationship.

Foundational to relationships is trust, and more often than not, trust is established through communication (verbal and non-verbal). For couples to maintain or establish trust in a relationship, it is vital to always keep in mind that only 7% of all communication is the actual words we use to communicate our message. The other 93% is our body language (55%) and our tone of voice (38%). This means, just because you didn't say something with your mouth, it doesn't mean you haven't said it with your body or eyes. Or if you said a seemingly level-headed thing with your mouth, but in an ugly tone, like, "Do what you want!" *(insert eye roll),* it doesn't actually mean someone should do as they wish. It means you're hurt and emotionally drained, and if that person does what they want, you'd be even more devastated.

We often don't communicate our true feelings because they are so closely connected to us that they stir fear and pain; two emotions we definitely don't want to deal with especially when we're not feeling accepted or loved to begin with.

Of course, if we communicated clearly: "This is hurting me because of x-y-z," then the other person can easily understand our position. However, being vulnerable enough to express our deepest hurt requires trust in our relationship so we can feel safe and open up. We also have to recognize our true feelings to be able to accurately express them, instead of jumping into instinctive defensive behaviours.

Therefore, the first step towards learning to communicate is to acknowledge your pain and hurt within. This will help stop you from projecting internal discomfort through aggressive words, tone, or body language.

Gender Differences in Communication

With an "across the board" type of statement, men are not inclined to hear "excessive" information, yet it's in a woman's nature to want to talk things out with details that men fail to absorb. It would be unkind to ask either one to change their ways but understanding goes a long way. Keeping these differences in mind can stop us from feeling triggered when our thoughts and discussions aren't received in the way we would have liked.

It's natural for women to generally want to talk things out and to be more expressive about how they feel, exactly when they feel it. Women commonly complain and become frustrated that their husbands don't meet them with the same enthusiasm and sharing or they simply "don't want to talk." It can be perceived as a form of rejection and can be a very painful point in the marriage. This is not to say that men don't also have similar experiences, but this view is expressed by women more often than not. Perhaps this point of contention comes from differing interests resulting in the same frustration and distance.

On the flip side, men are typically known as "fixers," especially those committed to creating a happy marital life. They want to help, make things better and feel whenever they speak or are spoken to by their womenfolk, it means they need to offer a solution. These men are on a mission to protect and care for their families. They are programmed to want to make things right, even if their wife is simply expressing herself with the only objective of getting it out of her mind. For many men, the need to swoop in and save the day is their way of expressing their love (even if he seems frustrated, and she doesn't feel loved by it). Many men interpret expressed emotions and sentiments as if it now becomes his responsibility, even though that's not the case.

Men tend to speak more purposefully, and they feel more vulnerable when getting into emotional conversations. Don't misunderstand me; men crave the security and space to open up, but it has to be in their time and on their terms. If they feel pressured by complaints or arguing, it will only keep them back longer and unmotivated to "just talk."

There is no right or wrong; there are merely differences to bear in mind so we aren't quickly offended when reactions aren't what we'd hope they would be.

When Communicating Fails

Logic dictates that if we explain ourselves, we'll open the doors to understanding, solve our problems, and everything will be peachy. Yet even when we do that, with a well-laid-out script in our head, it backfires and just makes things worse.

Unfortunately, it's easy to believe that we're fully in control of our emotions, and worse, that we're actually expressing them correctly. In reality, when we end up trying to "explain" or bring forth an understanding, it's done through raised voices, eye-rolling, crossed arms, frowning, etc. It's a hostile tone of voice and body language. No one surrounded by that demeanour will feel safe from being personally attacked and will likely automatically become defensive with their guard up high. It's likely if there's already tension, your partner is already on the defence.

When the level of trust in the relationship is already shaky, you can intend the nicest things possible, but the other person's interpretation will be negative. This is why creating trust, and therefore security, is so crucial for a healthy marriage.

Human nature (fear) leads us to confront our problems and pains with this type of hostility, but there is a better way. A way in which we'll not only feel better, but we'll get the results we were hoping for.

A beautiful lesson: The Prophet Muhammad, peace and blessings be upon him, gave his wife Aisha, may Allah be pleased with her, some advice: In Madinah, a group of people from a Jewish tribe entered upon the Prophet, peace and blessings be upon him, and said, "As-Samu'alayk (death be upon you)." He, peace and blessing be upon him, replied, "And upon you," but Aisha felt compelled to add, "Death be upon you, along with the curse of Allah and His wrath!"

The Messenger of Allah, peace and blessings be upon him, said, "O' Aisha, **be gentle! Indeed, Allah is gentle and loves gentleness in all matters. Beware of being harsh and vulgar.**" She said, "Did you not hear what they said?" He replied, "Did you not hear what I replied? I have returned their statement to them, except that my invocation against them will be accepted, while theirs against me will not be accepted."[32]

When we become conscious of our body language and the tone used when we communicate with our spouse, we will manifest the outcome we had hoped for. Of course, from our beloved Prophet's advice, peace and blessings be upon him, being gentle will create a place of security. It will also lessen any hostility due to our defence system going up. So, rather than defaulting to our intuitive nature (absentminded communication), which leads to unintentional self-sabotage, let's try to be mindful and gentle in the way we communicate with our spouse (even when we're annoyed).

Keep in mind, being gentle does not mean that you're not upset or hurt. It just means you won't project your pain to try to make the other person "feel it" too.

You're Human, Expect to Slip Up

Realistically, you have to expect that you aren't always going to be in control of how you're communicating, nor is your partner. Sometimes, while you're in the moment, you'll behave defensively and be triggered into an outburst of emotions, even if it isn't necessarily a representation of your true feelings. At some point, you'll also likely hurt (or offend) each other, but the idea here isn't perfection. The point is to develop security and comfort through gentleness such that it can sustain times when we are not our best selves.

First off, you must learn to be kind to yourself. Beating yourself up and making yourself feel terrible for a mistake will only take you back down and make you feel powerless over your actions. Accept that there will be times when you will slip but be quick to make amends by apologizing for your shortcomings (even if your reaction can be justified on some level).

---

[32] Al-Bukhari - 410, 6528

Be gentle in your apology and offer it with humility. Consider something like: "I'm sorry - I never want to hurt you, or ever wish hurt on you. Even if that's what happened, know I didn't mean any harm." For your spouse to be reminded of this, it will repair any foundational cracks and do wonders to your relationship. The fear of blame will disappear, and everyone's battle gear will be lowered, so that that constructive communication can happen. Taking individual responsibility will become the norm in your relationship - Insha'Allah. It also closes the doors to the whispering of Shaytaan, such as "He/She doesn't care about me," "That's his/her true feelings finally coming out!" etc.

Overcommunicating

Many have heard this over (and over!): "the key to a successful marriage is communication" - but is it?

While it is true on one level since understanding, empathy, and compromise require a level of communication, I would argue that this marital advice needs some serious context.

Unfortunately, the emphasis on marital communication is now often misunderstood to mean couples need to voice every thought they have ever had. Ever. In the past, it was common for both husband and wife to limit their opinions, but over time it created a gap between the two. One cannot know what another is feeling or thinking unless they express it. As well, one's partner cannot be faulted for something they do not know. Yet, this advice has been taken to an extreme with the misconception that marriage means a couple merges as though they are one mind, obligated to know everything. Some spouses even feel offended if their partner does not share this sentiment, despite their partner preferring to keep their internal dialogue to themselves.

All we own are our thoughts, and once they leave, we are no longer in control of them or what people do with them. Thoughts are very personal. They are very deeply connected to our sense of self and are naturally expressed when real intimacy is established within a marriage (i.e., trust, respect, honour, kindness, understanding, compassion, and sacrifice).

Expressing *all* your thoughts and emotions can be counterproductive to a healthy marriage because it can lead to controlling behaviours, with feelings of being suffocated by your partner's opinions. It can also create self-doubt in your spouse which eventually causes one or both to shut down. Also, the effects of over-communicating can be negatively perceived because unclear thoughts can be overwhelming to the listener, especially if this is done excessively.

Communication in a marriage is a balancing act. Of course, we don't want to have to filter ourselves or feel scared if we choose to express our thoughts or emotional states, including the ones the other person might not be comfortable hearing. However, overcommunicating too many ideas (especially if they are very scattered, unclear thoughts) can confuse one's spouse. A possible approach to keeping things clear, open, and still very much true to your natural self is to either choose to say something that serves a purpose of some sort or state your intention when you begin (i.e., I'm feeling confused and overwhelmed, I just want to say everything that's inside even if it doesn't make sense, don't worry if it doesn't make sense to you either). While this can feel like it's overkill (and strange) at first, in expressing your understanding of your partner's position, they can still feel included in your life. But at the same time not feel obliged to take responsibility or try to resolve your confusion.

"O you who believe! Keep your duty to Allah and fear Him, and speak (always) the truth." *(Quran 33:70)*

Undercommunicating

... *"I have no expectations!"*

Let's face it, not everyone is comfortable communicating their needs, especially (but not necessarily) if they have experienced rejection at some point in their life because of it. Communication can make some individuals feel vulnerable, therefore requiring a lot of mental work to muster up the strength to say what they want or need. Some people stop expressing their wants and needs because they feel they may be considered pushy, or feel they are insignificant and unworthy. Some feel they might be rejected or that by speaking up, they will be pushing their partner away, possibly even angering them, while others might just feel silly.

Asking for something can be very difficult for certain people, but truth be told, if you aren't able to ask, it creates a lot of lingering tension in the marriage. Just because a person doesn't express their needs or emotions, it doesn't mean that they don't have it, and most importantly, that they aren't valid.

There are some people that "cope" with unmet needs (sometimes expressed, but nothing comes of it) by choosing to "have no expectations." In having no expectations, you have not actually found a real solution. Instead, it is a defence mechanism to avoid disappointment (which rarely ever holds up). The truth is, you'll always have some level of expectations, whether you verbalize them or not. By "accepting everything" (i.e., not expressing your thoughts in a kind, courageous way), you're actually allowing it to fester within, resulting in an eventual, heightened argument.

Nonetheless, despite what we think, those unspoken words will come out eventually, but often in ugly ways. Sometimes in an explosive fit, sometimes in a passive-aggressive nagging way, sometimes it may just be this constant feeling of annoyance towards your partner without fully knowing why (body language).

Pushing things away because they are difficult to deal with never makes problems go away. When these non-verbalized expectations go unfulfilled, it leads to unfair blaming. When we don't take responsibility for our own selves and our own emotions, then blame likes to show its mean face. We unjustly blame our spouses because we are convinced that if we can fulfill their needs without them asking, then they should be able to do that for us too, right? Unfortunately, Allah has not given them the same intuitive nature to fulfill needs without being asked. Most of the time, spouses are oblivious to the fact that they aren't doing something that their partner would like but fails to express. If it were made known, they would likely have loved to help, care, nurture, love and be loved by fulfilling their spouse's needs. The responsibility is on each individual to keep the door open and not to shut their spouse out by "having no expectations."

Expressing our needs is a healthy habit as it establishes expectations, a very important element in a marriage, for you and your partner. Expectations set a standard in your relationship that each spouse can aim towards. It gives guidance, and it allows the opportunity for you to grow together. Don't worry, if at some point your requests seem unheard, still continue to express them. Try to excuse your spouse for their inability (for whatever reason) to fulfill them: possibly they just didn't "get it," or maybe they were going through their own thing, etc. Try to keep communication open, despite any feelings of rejection in the past. For those that are cringing at the thought of doing this, consider writing down your needs first so you, too, can make sense of them.

The effectiveness of setting expectations in a marriage is determined by how realistic you are. You can't expect your spouse to be someone they aren't just because that's what you want. However, you can definitely express your needs (without feeling like a burden) and try to come to a compromise. For example, just say your favourite pastime is spending time with your spouse, but maybe they best enjoy their own space. A compromise would be setting a fixed time (a day or two, or once a day) just for you two to catch up. This way, you get what you want, and they get what they want. Perhaps you'd like your spouse to bring home a surprise gift once in a while. You can't honestly expect them to know this is your desire unless you tell them. So, speak to one another openly, even if expressing this somewhat defeats the purpose of "surprise" (at least the first time).

Seek a balanced approach to your needs based on your knowledge of each other.

Those who have trouble asking, know that it will require some extra courage and will seem like work, but this is why a healthy marriage doesn't "just happen." We will all find certain things difficult, but they are necessary to establish an honest relationship and cultivate a sense of harmony between each other.

If this isn't you, but you know your spouse has a hard time asking or feels like a burden, then do your part by asking your spouse what you can do for them. Make it easy for your spouse to express their needs by opening yourself up to them and seeking that information. Keep reaffirming your desire to try to do whatever it is that will make them happy and remind them that they are not a burden or silly for saying how they feel. This might require a level of courage if you feel awkward easily, but in the long run, it's an easier option.

When spouses don't share their needs and resolve to "not expect anything," know the marriage will get dark at some point. We all have needs and wants, so if we keep our hearts open by seeking and actively wanting to fulfill our spouse's expectations, we will have also kept the doors to true intimacy open, Insha'Allah (and fewer problems).

Miscommunication Happens

When our thoughts and emotions are all over the place, we put marriage at risk of unnecessary strain. We inadvertently create a problem that never existed, but it often comes pouring out because we're confused ourselves and are trying to justify our emotions.

Therefore, it would be in the best interest for both partners to seek out a very trustworthy friend to open up to. Be very particular about who you choose to confide in. Look for those that have proven that they are rooting for you. Also, look for those you feel are conscious of Allah so they direct you towards goodness, even if what they advise is difficult for you to hear.

Once you have clarity about what you're feeling (thinking) and why you think that way, even a possible solution (but not necessarily), then go ahead and calmly talk it out with your spouse. Try to clear your mind and open your heart to each other.

What if there is no one you trust enough to talk to? Then what?

Write it down.

You can always rip it up when you're done but put it in writing. It will help you to verbalize your thoughts, pull out whatever is untrue and focus on what you know to be good and true (this will all become apparent as you write, Insha'Allah).

Keep your words truthful and keep them concise. The more excessive one is in speech, the more likely emotions and scenarios get distorted opening the way to unnecessary blow-ups.

Do note: Truthful doesn't mean nasty. If you're still feeling bitter, then you'll distort the truth with those negative emotions.

Guard Your Secrets

While I just finished saying that it might benefit us to sometimes turn to a trustworthy friend, I do not advocate going to a friend every time there is a bump in the marriage. It's a wise practice to keep people at arm's length from your marriage. My suggestion for you to confide in someone trustworthy should only be done for major conflicts that require clarity and are very painful for you. Both men and women need someone to talk to other than each other when these inevitable conflicts arise. They aren't deal-breakers; they are merely building blocks to a healthier, more balanced marriage.

Keep in mind, even when ranting about your marital issue(s) to a family member or a friend, there must always be a level of discretion. Your purpose is to find a solution, not validation. Thus, offering unnecessary details that simply make someone look bad or are very private is unacceptable. You are still talking about your spouse - your garment. At that moment, you may be upset, but always protect their honour and dignity as you would like for yourself.

You will forgive and move on at some point, but that doesn't mean the person you're confiding in feels the same way. They may formulate opinions and become harsh with your spouse, which may cause unnecessary tension. Choose who you confide in wisely.

The Prophet, peace and blessings be upon him, said: "The most wicked among the people in the eye of Allah on the Day of Judgment are the men who goes to his wife and she comes to him, and then he divulges her secret."[33]

---

[33] Sahih Muslim 1437 a - Book 8, Hadith 3369

Grow × Learn × Live

Learn to discuss any problems in your marriage by speaking straight to the point. Trying to tiptoe around issues creates a lot of confusion and often entails saying too much or too little then what's necessary.

Try to be balanced in your discussion and accept each other's natures without wanting your spouse to be your clone.

When times are hard, find a trustworthy friend to confide in. Your objective is to look for the truth of the matter. Also, always keep this in mind: you and your spouse are still on the same team (even if it doesn't feel that way)!

Chapter 15 – Forgiving

Seeking Forgiveness and Saying Sorry

Forgiveness is a very broadly used term and needs to be defined in the context of marriage, especially in an Islamic marriage.

As you know, each spouse is granted God-given rights, which, as believers, obligates us to fulfill. If a spouse fails to uphold any of the rights upon him or her, then they would be considered sinful. In engaging in repentance to Allah for this sin, they have to first ask for forgiveness from their spouse. The person wronged is not obligated to forgive, but if they do, then it is better for them. However, just because someone chooses to forgive does not imply that they no longer feel hurt. It means that before Allah, the one who transgressed is in the clear with respect to the person they wronged.

Also, bear in mind that there is a distinct difference between willingly giving up rights and rights that are transgressed. The former entails their partner excused them of fulfilling certain right(s), while the latter necessitates forgiveness is sought for failing to fulfill what is due, as it is a transgression of Allah's laws.

Intertwined within this topic is the issue of hurt feelings, which may not have anything to do with rights per se nor with the need to seek forgiveness from a spiritual (repentance) point of view. It could simply mean the other person was offended, perhaps because they were triggered by a past event that may have nothing to do with you. It entails apologizing to establish kindness, mercy, compassion, and empathy which will soften hearts, therefore exercising good character. Ultimately that is also a right - good conduct.

It's important to distinguish between the rights owed, rights pardoned, and taking personal offence because to seek forgiveness takes on a spiritual connotation. In contrast, an apology doesn't necessarily have religious implications.

Forgiveness is contingent upon a transgression of rights. An apology, however, is due to an offence.

for·give	a·pol·o·gy
to grant pardon for or remission of (an offence, debt, etc.); absolve.	a regretful acknowledgment of an offence or failure.

Addressing Hurt Feelings

Hurt feelings can happen by accident, such as a husband forgetting that his wife had asked him to help her with something that she deemed important or a wife accidentally washing her husband's favourite white thobe with a red towel turning it pink. In both instances, a spouse can potentially become very upset. Yet in both scenarios, neither were intentional acts of wanting to harm or wronging their spouse. They are innocent mistakes.

Even if one's intent was not to hurt their spouse, their partner may feel hurt or offended (likely due to a deeper issue in the marriage which often makes their displeasure seem petty). Despite one's intent, an apology is warranted as it re-establishes the fact that no harm was meant by such an error.

The act of saying sorry and accepting the apology as a means of amends requires both parties to elevate in character: one to find the humility to say sorry even though it can easily not be seen as a "fault" by someone else, and the other to accept it as a mistake by not holding negative feelings or a grudge because of it (just as you would want them to do for you when you make a mistake).

Our many experiences in life come together to construct the complexities of our own self. Things one would laugh at, another might be deeply hurt by. Simply because one has experienced pain similar to what was expressed, thereby causing them to feel triggered (possibly from a past negative experience with you or perhaps by no fault of your own). Rarely is it a spouse's intention to hurt their partner, yet it still happens. Unfortunately, if things escalate, partners become defensive, put up emotional walls, and things get nasty for no good reason.

Obviously, even unintentionally hurting your spouse's feelings still creates conflict, but it doesn't warrant asking for forgiveness; it warrants an apology. A heartfelt apology will reinforce that your intent was never to hurt or harm them. Compassion and forgiveness go hand-in-hand in creating a loving, healthy marriage.

Overlooking faults, saying sorry, and accepting an apology are all acts of forgiving and are essential components in a marriage, which without, a marriage will always be on the rocks. As humans, we will always have faults, and while it's good to try to avoid offending each other, at some point, we will all be guilty of it. Remembering that these offences are unintentional will help one move forward and not allow inevitable mistakes to define the relationship.

When a relationship lacks emotional security, then any small behaviour (even chewing!) can cause each other to be offended, with little or no reason. The quicker you are to "feel hurt," the greater the indication of instabilities within the relationship. So, fixing problems in the marriage will require a more in-depth understanding than merely saying sorry.

If you find yourself often offended or offending your partner, it is typical a symptom of one's fears: the fear of betrayal or abandonment, the fear of loss; be it financial or personal, the fear of one's insecurities being true, and so on. It helps to keep this in mind because when petty issues arise, they can escalate, and neither husband or wife know why they are feeling so upset, except that, to them, their spouse is mean or an idiot.

While "being upset" for a long period gives us a false sense of security (thinking we're protecting ourselves), it doesn't actually give us what we want (peace and comfort in our marriage). Holding onto hurt is behaviour that will self-sabotage, causing us more pain than any incident ever warrants.

Transgression of Rights

No marriage is free from offences and unintentionally hurting the feelings of each other; it's inevitable. However, when issues stem from a transgression of rights: food, shelter, good treatment, intimacy etc., then the scar of such effects runs deep. Our basic needs are safeguarded in the rights that are owed to us in marriage, Alhamdulilah! Unfortunately, when a transgression of rights occur, the road to recovery is long. There is no "edit undo." Nothing can be undone, only to forgive, but they are rarely ever forgotten.

Forgiveness in a marriage is fundamental to moving forward positively, but it takes unearthing the layers of pain for this to sincerely manifest. As we learn to understand the nature of forgiving and how embracing it has positive effects on us (more than our spouse), this journey becomes easier.

For many dealing with painful moments simply means "out of sight" (never discussed), but internally it breeds ugly thoughts. Feelings are kept hidden with the twisted (but instinctive) logic that by not putting our guard down (or "forgetting), we are protecting ourselves from hurting again. In reality, all we are doing is constantly refreshing and caressing the pain over and over again. Therefore, this "protection" is being nourished so that it can live as long as we do!

If you are the one that has transgressed your spouse's rights, remember, you are not "guilty for life," and no one has the right to make you feel that way either. Seek forgiveness from your spouse, and turn to Allah, the Most Forgiving, Most Merciful! At the same time, don't dismiss that your actions created turmoil in your partner, as that is throwing contaminated salt to the wound (i.e., it won't heal, only sting, and further become infected). Your best bet is to make a continuous effort to re-establish trust and build safety in your marriage by addressing your spouse's insecurities that your actions unveiled and pushed into overdrive.

Also, to help initiate reconciliation after feelings of hurt or a transgression of rights, you must always keep in mind that you are on the same team. Your spouse is not your enemy, even if they can be selfish, inconsiderate, mean, rude, annoying, and any negative trait you can think of. Each one, equally, will likely be all of these traits, plus some, at some moment or another. However, it does not define your marriage because no one is perfect - the reader and definitely the writer included!

Why Forgive?

> "And the men of grace and wealth among you should not swear against giving (their charitable gifts) to the kinsmen and the poor and to those who have migrated in the way of Allah. **And they**

should forgive and forego. Do you not like that Allah forgives you? And Allah is Most-Forgiving, Very-Merciful." *(Quran 24:22)*

Dr. Fred Luskin, author of *Forgive for Love,* has created an entire program related to forgiveness. He teaches that "Forgiveness is the experience of being at peace in the present." According to him, life happened, and we objected to such events, hence it created emotional, physical, and spiritual turmoil within ourselves. Therefore, he says, "Forgiveness is making peace when you don't get what you want."

> "No disaster strikes except by the permission of Allah. And whoever believes in Allah - He will guide his heart. And Allah is Knowing of all things." *(Quran 64:11)*

The Prophet, peace and blessings be upon him, reminds us of the importance of accepting decree is this hadith: "A strong believer is better and is more lovable to Allah than a weak believer, and there is good in everyone, (but) cherish that which gives you benefit (in the Hereafter) and seek help from Allah and do not lose heart, and if anything (in the form of trouble) comes to you, don't say: If I had not done that, it would not have happened so and so, but say: Allah did that what He had ordained to do and your 'if' opens the (gate) for the Satan."[34]

    Essentially, we are offended, hurt, or bothered by others simply because we are experiencing emotional turmoil. We prefer to blame instead of forgive, pardon, or overlook because we lack peace inside ourselves. Interestingly enough, Islam means "submission to the will of God," and it is derived from the Arabic word "salaam," which means peace. It is to submit to our circumstances, knowing that Allah is in control and that whatever happens in our life is intended specifically for us. As believers, we know with certainty that there is good in everything; hence submission is directly related to peace.
    When we learn to truly submit, we establish peace within ourselves and can forgive.

---

[34] Sahih Muslim 2664 - Book 33, Hadith 6441

Forgiving, letting go, overlooking, moving on - whatever you want to call it - does not invalidate our feelings of hurt, but instead it empowers us to go beyond a moment of pain and live freely. It is human nature and absolutely natural to feel hurt, even angry. Therefore, how you forgive should also display a level of mercy and compassion to yourself.

The Messenger of Allah, peace and blessings be upon him, said, "Strange are the ways of a believer for there is good in every affair of his and this is not the case with anyone else except in the case of a believer for if he has an occasion to feel delight, he thanks (God), thus there is a good for him in it, and if he gets into trouble and shows resignation (and endures it patiently), there is a good for him in it."[35]

What Does 'Forgiving' Look Like?

Forgiveness towards your spouse has many layers because normally an offence evokes various emotions; possibly mistrust, contempt, bitterness, doubt, or downright soul-crushing pain. You begin to question what you thought you once knew about your spouse, whether it's their character, their love, their presence in your life, etc. Depending on what has transpired in your marriage, there can be many levels of disappointment.

Kimberly Yates breaks it down like this, "Forgiveness starts with truth, ushered in with love and leads to freedom."

Consider starting the process of clearing your heart and finding a sense of peace by doing the following:

1. Clearly and specifically state the offense[36]

Tell yourself, loud and clear, what precisely happened and what exactly about that situation hurt you so much. In this process, you learn to "fact find" and to determine if your interpretation of events (thoughts) is genuinely yours or are actually the whisperings of Shaytaan trying to cause discord.

---

[35] Sahih Muslim 2999 - Book 42, Hadith 7138
[36] Kimberly Yates

Ask "what" questions: What was my role? What would I have liked to happen? What does my response mean? What do I want to achieve? What would I do differently? What can they do differently? Etc.

2. Clearly communicate your findings

Let your partner know what you just learned about yourself – how you felt, and why you felt that way. This gives them the opportunity to grow and learn about you because, more likely than not, their actions were not intentional (as I keep reiterating because we often want to believe otherwise to try to justify our hurt).

3. **Let it go**

Regardless if you get an apology or not, you should now be equipped with the truth of the matter. Let it go without bitterness left in your heart. That bitterness will destroy you, and no one, not even your beloved spouse, should have that type of control over you (unleashing your "dark side" and starting to hate who you are becoming). Holding onto these negative emotions deludes you into thinking you've avoided getting (hurt) again because by holding on, you will continuously be chained to this pain, to the point that it'll start to define you. Remember that this is your husband or your wife, and you have a family and home together. Show compassion to your companion because that's what it takes to be a garment to one another. Two hurts won't heal any wounds; they will only just keep ripping open wider!

4. **Keep it in the past**

We hang onto things as a defensive mechanism. Of course, you won't forget, but every experience, even if it's negative, is designed to teach us a lesson. When the lesson is learned, put it behind you. You need not hold onto it thinking it's keeping you safe. It's not.

5. Make du'aa (supplication)

Make du'aa for yourself and make du'aa for your spouse. A saving grace for you when battling the tests of life is the more someone hurts you, the more du'aa you should make for them. The reason? Hurt has the potential to make our heart hard, and a hardened heart is a big problem for us in this world and the hereafter. We should want to viciously protect our heart from becoming hard. So, one way to soften our heart it is to make du'aa for others, especially those that may have hurt us in some way.

6. Trust Allah

Allah hears and is aware of all things. Perhaps in the moment, your spouse can't see why you're hurt, yet you make a choice to overlook their error and their suggestion that you are "wrong," "crazy," or even "dramatic" to feel the way you feel (i.e., hurt). Allah knows your experiences and why you're hurting, so trust that He will make your affairs right. Even if others seem not to understand you, Allah is near and knows all.

Here is an incentive for the believer to forgive and a reminder that life is littered with opportunities to do good deeds (Insha'Allah):

"And hasten towards forgiveness from your Lord and a paradise as vast as the heavens and the earth, prepared for those mindful (of Allah). (They are) those who donate in prosperity and adversity, control their anger, and pardon others. And Allah loves the good-doers." *(Quran 3:133-134)*

Chapter 16 – Resolution
When Stuck in Conflict

> "O you who have believed, seek help through patience and prayer. Indeed, Allah is with the patient." *(Quran 2:153)*

In a relationship, conflict or the "contraction stage" recycles the same issues repeatedly, typically stemming from the first few times the relationship went through this cycle. It's normal for many couples to reach a point where they find themselves feeling "stuck" - there are no more conversations that need to be had, there are no more strategies that they can come up with, and there are no compromises that they can deploy to fix things. When this happens, couples often separate unless they choose to endure the situation.

So, what then is the answer?

"The answer comes when we realize that the effort to remain stable requires constant change, and that every change requires new efforts to remain stable."[37]

Instead of merely enduring each other, a couple can learn to give up blaming and bitterness. After all, it is only with seemingly new information that someone will feel empowered to come out of the contraction stage and attempt to make amends. Perhaps this change of heart is triggered by a traumatic event, loss of a loved one, or knowledge they never heard or understood before. Either way, the realization and acceptance that we cannot change anyone but ourselves empowers a couple to move past adverse circumstances. It also helps when we learn to give up trying to get what we want through constant demands, emotional abuse, and various other manipulative tactics. Instead, we choose to focus our energies on self-rectification.

Through the pain that conflict unearths, couples can harness the strength to transform their condition, especially if they are patient enough to get past the heartache and turn to Allah in prayer.

As hard as times become, don't give up hope. Know the defining difference between moving forward and calling it quits or staying

---
[37] Dr. Barry Dym and Dr. Michael L. Glenn - *Couples*

debilitated in your relationship is information. Information transforms your condition because it allows for insight, options, and emotional security to change your perspective.

So, take a deep breath and be honest with yourself first. If you are two good people who have shared some amazing times together, trust that with time, knowledge, reflection, and patience, better days are ahead – Insha'Allah.

> "Still, these couples who survive and thrive through today's arduous journey strike us as having achieved something astonishing. There is something heroic about people who have the capacity to sustain crushing disappointment, undergo repeated tests of their relationship, and still feel enhanced by their commitment to each other."[38]

Reaching Out

In earlier chapters, I discussed the idea of reaching out to someone trustworthy from time-to-time, if necessary, to help resolve issues that creep up. However, sometimes it's not bumps you're looking to climb over but mountains that seem impossible to overcome. In cases like this, when hope seems lost, we are given instructions in finding a way through.

> "If you fear a breach between them twain (the man and his wife), appoint (two) arbitrators, one from his family and the other from hers; if they both wish for reconciliation, Allah will cause their reconciliation. Indeed, Allah is Ever All-Knower, Well-Acquainted with all things." *(Quran 4:35)*

Bringing a person from each side of the family will allow for just perspectives. It will also offer the couple new information based on varying perceptions, and it will work to establish accountability within the relationship. Of course, be sure that the people you involve in your marriage all share the same objective of wanting reconciliation.

With a third and fourth party in the mix, there is someone else that is looking, that is judging, that has expectations, that is putting their

---

[38] Dr. Barry Dym and Dr. Michael L. Glenn - *Couples*

trust in your word, that is rooting for your success etc. Having those extra people involved when you cannot resolve matters on your own will create a level of accountability. It is also beneficial in gaining a balanced perspective and mending ties – Insha'Allah.

Re-Establishing Leadership for Resolution

Dr. Robert Nay, a clinical psychologist and expert in anger management, says, "most people's conditions for resolve are irrational."

Therefore, meeting people's conditions isn't necessarily the most realistic solution as sometimes their conditions are even impossible. As believers, we have to take everything back to our beloved Prophet's ways, peace and blessing be upon him, and the laws in which Islam is established.

Therefore, finding a resolution or even needing to "give in" in order to establish a sense of peace in the home is much easier done when we fully understand who has the final say, or rather who has the right. In Islam, the right of leadership in the home is the husband's, to the extent that a wife is to obey whatever he decides even if he doesn't exercise wisdom in consultation, provided that what he is demanding is not haram (forbidden).

The following verse sums up the mentality we should have because, the truth is, we aren't always going to like the situation we're in. We may even hate it because it feels awkward or uncomfortable, but that doesn't mean it's bad for us or harming us.

> "... it may be that you dislike a thing which is good for you and that you like a thing which is bad for you. Allah knows but you do not know." *(Quran 2:216)*

It is not a requirement to understand and find reason in the commands of Allah before we obey.

The believer says,

> "...We hear, and we obey. (We seek) Your Forgiveness, our Lord, and to You is the return (of all)." *(Quran 2:285)*

In achieving a balanced understanding, we should keep in mind that accompanied by the husband's greater degree in authority is also a much greater responsibility – one that he is obligated to answer for before Allah. This entails that his account before Allah is greater, and he should not take these rights of responsibilities lightly.

There is justice in everything our religion teaches, so for us to hold to this concept of "equality" based on a Western perspective is to undermine the wisdom and perfection of our Master.

The Messenger of Allah, peace and blessings be upon him, said, "Every one of my Ummah will enter Jannah except those who refuse." He was asked: "Who will refuse?'" He, peace and blessings be upon him, said, "Whoever obeys me, shall enter Jannah, and whosoever disobeys me, refuses to (enter Jannah)."[39]

That said, if a man fulfills the rights upon him, he will see the rewards pouring forth for him on the only day that matters - the Day of Judgement.

When Rights Are All You Have

When you are stuck in your marriage and can't seem to see any light at the end of the tunnel, then strip away the promises, the pain, the feeling of loneliness or rejection, etc. Start afresh by re-establishing your intention and understand why you are doing what you're doing.

"In resolution, partners stop imposing their will on each other."[40]

When we can begin to centre ourselves with the right intention, we also choose better actions, better words, and better body language. Otherwise, the imbalance within can quickly lead to a downward spiral.

---

[39] Al- Bukhari - Riyad Al-Salihin 158 - Hadith 158
[40] Dr. Barry Dym and Dr. Michael L. Glenn - *Couples*

Keep this verse from Surah Rahman in mind:

"Is the reward for good [anything] but good?" *(Quran 55:60)*

Divorce is a reality that is increasingly more common as the days go by. Divorce doesn't happen because one or both partners are "bad" (sometimes it does, but it doesn't account for the steady rise in divorce rates). It happens because we don't know how to handle the situations that we find ourselves in.

The stage of resolution is where both partners find peace in their situation. There isn't any resentment or internal discord. Why? Because they "stop imposing their will on each other" (i.e., control).

The Honoured Wife

A woman's role in resolution is vital because she sets the stage in how she chooses to manifest her presence: "happy wife, happy life" – has some truth to it! Unfortunately, this can be a very mentally and emotionally draining role to play. As such, we can sometimes lose sight of the end goal and lose out on the very same thing(s) we desire, in this world and the hereafter.

Marriage for women offers us an excellent opportunity to come closer to Allah. Even in doing those mundane tasks, we are earning rewards and elevating our status. Serving our families is a noble act and a difficult one too. Society has downgraded the status of a wife and mother with the question, "What do you do all day?" or "Is that all you do?" – the implication is that a woman has not achieved much in upholding the role of a wife.

Any woman committed to the needs of her family knows that it is beyond a full-time job. Allah is just! A man may see a tangible reward for serving his family, but a woman may get nothing physical in return (no paycheques or employee-of-the-month award). However, Allah has promised the righteous woman great honour. There's not a career in this world that can ever come close to the reward of a righteous wife.

As arduous as a wife and mother's duty can be, always keep your eye on the prize because before you know it, we will all be before our Creator. If it means a little hardship, annoyance, discomfort, whining, so be it – Jannah is worth it! There is no greater motivation for a woman in her role as a wife than this:

The Messenger of Allah, peace and blessings be upon him, said, "Any woman dies while her husband is pleased with her, she will enter Jannah."[41]

> ## Grow × Learn × Live
> Do not be afraid of conflict. Realize all it means is that you are due for some fine-tuning. Be open to change and turn to Allah. Redirect your emotional state. Beg Allah to give you the strength and wisdom to overcome the negative emotions you are feeling and grant you clarity through truth in the situation.

---

[41] Al-Tirmidhi - Riyad Al-Salihin 286 - Hadith 286

Chapter 17 – Happy Marriages

When Marriages Thrive

So... what is a happy marriage anyway?!

A happy marriage is characterized by healthy patterns of behaviour that lead to both partners feeling satisfied. These are learned behaviours that take time to fully develop because you have to first get to know one another. Making the necessary effort to learn and implement positive behaviours in your marriage is what is meant by "putting in the work."

Unfortunately, much of the efforts couples put into trying to "fix the problem" often leads to both of them still feeling frustrated and upset. It is common that both equally feel that they are "putting in the work" (and a lot of it!) but sadly, it's not effective. "Work" that consists of sour compromises, discussions in triggered states causing each other to "walk on eggshells," and so forth will not lead to marital satisfaction. These are Band-Aid type solutions don't stick because they are not focused on the real issues within the marriage, and more so, individually.

To sustain peace and comfort in your marriage, you and your spouse need to create a system that supports these outcomes (peace and comfort) rather than resort to default habits of interaction. Issues in a marriage are a manifestation of faults within this "system," such as reactions towards each other, expectations of how a relationship "should" function, and how you organize your roles within the relationship.

Pat Love's book, *5 Forces Destroying Your Marriage,* discusses how to create a stable and secure marriage based on fixing the system in which you both operate. She teaches that a successful marriage requires a couple's system to include five components: security, fairness, flexibility, relational, and alive. I'd like to add a sixth component to this system that should lead the way: putting Allah and His Messenger, peace and blessings be upon him, first, before your own self. In doing this, other components will fall more naturally into place.

How a Healthy System Looks

Since a healthy marriage is comprised of healthy patterns of behaviour, the reverse of it holds true too; an unhealthy marriage is from unhealthy patterns. These patterns are often developed over the first few years of marriage yet determine the next 60+ years. Fifty percent of marriages that end in divorce do so before the seventh year of marriage, which means that learning and correcting is especially necessary throughout the early years to create the stability required for a lasting, content marriage Insha'Allah.

1. Faith

> "O you who have believed, do not put [yourselves] before Allah and His Messenger but fear Allah. Indeed, Allah is Hearing and Knowing." *(Quran 49:1)*

It's natural and easy for emotions to run high in marriage. Feelings are not factual, nor can they see "the bigger picture," yet we more often than not act on how we feel. This instinct leads us to self-sabotage. Therefore, it's in our best interest to rely first on the manners we learn from our faith to dictate our reactions instead of relying on our emotions. In doing so, we will ensure that those minor bumps do not escalate into bigger, unnecessary problems. As such, we need to study the history of the Prophet, peace and blessings be upon him, and ahadith to grasp the essence of good character.

While we may strive to do our best, we must acknowledge that challenges will still be part of marriage, and we may not know how to deal with them, or we may choose to react in a way that creates a gap in the relationship. Therefore, as believers, our priority is to find solutions through Islamic teachings, whether we agree, can relate, understand, or even feel comfortable with them. An example of this is getting up for fajr salah. A majority of people don't feel like waking up before sunrise, but they do, and they do it to obey Allah. The same goes for a marriage. We follow the laws set forth for us, which ultimately offer the best solution to anything that comes our way.

Muslim marriages can quickly be balanced if the desire to please Allah is central to the relationship. Staying steadfast in this intention, with the knowledge we won't always be our best, is fundamental in creating a healthy marital system. It is also a strong strategy to keep Shaytaan out of our head and our marriage!

2. Security

Vulnerability is a huge component in developing closeness between couples. Unfortunately, while it offers a great reward, it can be challenging to do. When a marriage thrives, it provides a place of safety, so no one feels threatened, and each partner willingly seeks to lower their guarded self. Developing security means both partners are confident in a few things: they won't be judged, they're in this together, honesty won't create discord, and they can be themselves without being mocked or controlled. Spouses work with each other for the benefit of each other and their family. Essentially, it's working to secure each other's emotional, physical, financial, and sexual fidelity.

In other words, you are a garment to one another:

"…They are clothing for you and you are clothing for them…" *(Quran 2:187)*

Establishing a sense of safety within the marriage functions as a protective cover for each other's needs. Therefore, providing a place of emotional and physical shelter, as well as a source of warmth and comfort.

3. Fairness

Nothing quite tips the scales of balance than an unjust situation.

Both husband and wife have a fundamental role to play in their relationship and home. However, if one consistently chooses to sit back and "let things slide" and the other picks up the slack, over time, an unfair system is constructed in the marriage.

With fairness in a marriage, each partner is committed to putting in 100% of themselves. This means that even though each person's role will be different, and while one person at some point may be doing more than the other, there is no scorekeeping. Both partners approach marriage with confidence that the outcome will be equitable, and both tackle the work required with an equal commitment to the cause (family stability).

To establish fairness in your relationship, try to understand each other's expectations in an open, honest manner. Create a mutually acceptable game plan of what fairness would look like to each of you on a day-to-day basis. In respecting these mutually agreed roles and fulfilling the obligations upon you, with trust that Allah is just, fairness will be present in your union.

"O you who believe, fear Allah, and everybody must consider what he (or she) has sent ahead for tomorrow. And fear Allah. Surely Allah is fully aware of what you do." *(Quran 59:18)*

4. Flexibility

Marriage is a lifelong commitment, which means you have to expect that each of us will change along the way. We are not the same person we were ten years ago or even five. We learn, we grow, and hopefully, we get wiser along the way. Also, the circumstances surrounding a marriage will change: jobs, health, family situations, children and their needs, etc.

Everyone, at some point, questions their purpose, self-worth, role in life, meeting with Allah, etc. We reflect, absorb and journey through life differently from each other, despite the closeness we may have with our spouses. This causes us to change. Sometimes for the better and sometimes for the worse. A husband and wife need to learn to adapt to each other's differences, accept change without fear of loss (this is established when creating security), and embrace whatever is decreed.

In a healthy marriage, we readily adapt to these changes without any sense of resentment. Even if our spouse's character is a bit off or snappy, we accept it with an openness and a willingness to relearn their newer self.

Flexibility in marriage allows us to simply be human and experience a range of emotions without fear that our partner won't accept us. Of course, it isn't for us to accept haram (forbidden) acts and say, "well, they're just changing." Allah's law is first, and there's no messing about with that. However, within Islamic boundaries, we will still change, and those changes need to be embraced by one another rather than analyzed and criticized.

"In most successful couples, partners have the capacity to tolerate each other's change without taking it as a personal affront."[42]

As believers, we can better grasp the transient nature of this life, which better prepares us for the varying challenges to come our way. Anticipating these tests involves flexibility in schedules, roles, sacrifices, needs and wants. Therefore, to maintain stability, couples need to jointly accept the instability of circumstances and function as one team.

"Do people think that they will be left alone because they say: 'We believe,' and will not be tested. And We indeed tested those who were before them. And Allah will certainly make (it) known (the truth of) those who are true and will certainly make (it) known (the falsehood of) those who are liars, (although Allah knows all that before putting them to test)." *(Quran 29:2-3)*

5. Relational

I cannot stress enough how vital it is to your marriage to always consider yourselves as a team, on the same side, wanting the same things for the greater good of your family. It is essential to form a partnership. While each individual will have different roles, both are working to win the game: supporting, cheering, defending, and active until the game is over.

Creating a relational system means you work with the best interest of each other in mind, and ultimately, your family as a whole. That means whatever you do, you're actively aware that your actions have a direct impact on your spouse.

A simple example might be going to sleep late, which can result in oversleeping. Oversleeping will mean you can't fulfill your job of

---

[42] Dr. Barry Dym and Dr. Michael L. Glenn - *Couples*

taking the children to school in the morning. Either they will be late, or your partner has to scramble to take them. You didn't consider that you'll fall short in your responsibilities in sleeping late, and someone else would have to pick up the slack. Of course, we are all humans and mistakes happen, but if you or your spouse are constantly "dropping the ball," then it becomes a serious problem, and you cease to have a relational system in place. However, when mistakes or circumstances happen from time-to-time, and each spouse quickly swoops in to help, the system is relational. You are working as a team, without blaming.

Tiny scenarios of selfish actions that negatively affect the entire family can chip away at the structure of the marriage. It is no longer a partnership that works together but instead a burdensome load for one to carry alone.

A great reminder that supports the development of a relational partnership is found in our beautiful religion.

The Prophet Muhammad, peace and blessings of Allah be upon him, said: "None of you (truly) believes until he loves for his brother that which he loves for himself."[43]

6. Alive

Having a marriage that is alive requires you both to keep things interesting, fun, peaceful, spontaneous, and happy. If a marriage falls into the same mundane day-in and day-out activities, things will start feeling strained and tiring. Boredom is harsh on the mind and can lead to a great deal of negativity.

Changing the pace always helps to create some excitement and fun. Try things such as cooking a different meal or cooking together, rearranging furniture, getting a new outfit and revelling in it, going out for some ice cream, giving each other a foot massage, pulling out some board games, flirting with one another (however you do it!), playing a harmless prank on each other, telling knock-knock jokes, etc. Get creative! Marriage is fun if you allow it to be!

---

[43] Sahih Al-Bukhari 13 - Vol. 1, Book 2, Hadith 13

Once the Holy Prophet, peace and blessing be upon him, raced against Aisha, may Allah be pleased with her, while she was on a journey along with the Messenger of Allah, peace and blessings be upon him, she said: "I had a race with him (the Prophet), and I outstripped him on my feet. When I became fleshy, (again) I had a race with him (the Prophet) and he outstripped me." He, peace and blessings be upon him, said: "This is for that outstripping."[44]

Grow × Learn × Live

Reflect on the way your marriage functions. Try to adjust areas so it includes the (mentioned above) components of a healthy marital system. If you have all six areas as the foundation of your marriage, you'll be on your way to enjoying a beautiful marriage. A marriage that has its equal share of disagreements but can still gracefully overcome them – Insha'Allah.

---

[44] Sunan Abi Dawud 2578 - Book 14, Hadith 2572

Chapter 18 – Establishing Respect

Respect is Loving

Showing respect in a marriage can be the difference between a civil and workable union or bitter stubbornness. Respect softens the heart and is a seed from which true love blooms. Knowing if respect exists between a couple can quickly be observed in how they interact with each other. Without respect in a marriage, problems escalate dramatically, and communication ceases to benefit their relationship.

Respect does not control, and it does not try to be right either. It is also not manipulative, and it doesn't have an agenda. Respect says so much about you and nothing about the other person. It is not conditional; rather, it is the highest expression of manners.

The word "respect" is interpreted differently from culture to culture. However, I believe there are universal forms of respect that are fundamental to a marriage. In upholding them, a standard of interaction will always remain consistent within the relationship. I call them "Laws of Respect" (*how original, I know*). These unspoken "laws" are the boundaries of a healthy marriage that both parties should strive to maintain, regardless of what offences occurred in the past or present.

These laws can be tough to uphold when emotions run high, but we must internalize them as "laws." If they are broken, the consequence is pain and hurt in a marriage. In times of hurt or intense frustration, these rules will keep a marriage from turning one relatively small event into a disaster. It also offers a "security net" for communication to happen by setting an expected baseline.

To execute these laws, one would need to be conscious of their present state and keep a level head. Again, perfection is not the goal. Instead, as we learn a better way to interact, we begin to see its value and work harder to cultivate healthy habits within our marriage.

You won't always adhere to these "laws" but if you become willfully aware of them, you'll be on the path to creating healthy habits within your marriage, Insha'Allah.

Laws of Respect
Body Language – kindness
Tone of Voice – polite and controlled
Listening – don't have to accept, but try to understand, no arguing
Roles – Islamically-mandated positions of authority
Demeanour – non-judgemental, not controlling
Behaviour – express gratitude and positivity
Expectations – acceptance of truth and if you cannot agree, then choose to agree to disagree
Response – acceptance of the other's emotions and a willingness to fulfill their needs.

A husband and wife know each other very well, to the extent that the moment one starts doing things differently, the other will notice. Continue fixing things in your marriage so that you always adhere to these "Laws of Respect." You'll start seeing changes in the other person too, especially once they start feeling safe and secure (that this new-found respect is going to stay and not be a one-time event).

Is Respect Earned?

A lack of respect will add a lot of distance within a relationship. The intimacy that remains would be limited to physical needs but not emotional. The more times these laws of respect are transgressed, the further apart you'll become.

A follow-up thought that often arises with these rules is the idea that sometimes a person has transgressed in such a way that you no longer respect them. Keep in mind, how you treat a person is not dependent upon how they have treated you because of self-respect.

With self-respect, we hold ourselves with dignity and do what is honourable, despite what others choose to do. So, just because you choose to show someone respect, regardless of their attitude or actions, it does not mean that they deserve it. It just means you're in control of yourself.

Respect is not interchangeable with trust. If someone wronged you then yes, you may no longer trust them, but it's always your choice to show respect because that's the type of person you choose to be.

Boundaries Create Self-Respect

Sometimes going above and beyond your role within the marriage actually strips your partner of their own self-respect. Essentially, you're telling them that they can't manage their role within the marriage. This stripping of a person's sense of self-respect can even come in the form of micromanaging your partner or interacting with the mindset that there's only one "right" way to do something (your way!). This disrespectful gesture (though likely not intentionally disrespectful) is controlling and is often justified as "helping" or wanting to "make things easier" for the other person. In reality, we are dismissing our partner's position in the marriage (including their Islamic role) and creating a gap of insecurity in our partner.

Also, the person exceeding boundaries will eventually feel depleted and likely resentful over time, despite that this consequence is self-inflicted.

In respecting our spouse, it is essential we honour their personal space to do things the way they choose. This will keep them feeling free and safe from being judged or "helped" all the time. After all, it's in our nature to desire the feeling of having purpose and wanting to feel accomplished (proud of ourselves) through fulfilling our responsibilities.

Grow × Learn × Live

In creating peace and comfort in marriage, boundaries of respect have to be established. There's simply no way around it!

Grab a pen and paper and note which "laws" you tend to have a hard time sticking to. If you have three or more on your list, pick the first two that are the easiest to fix and keep repeating them to yourself. Force your brain to be conscious of them and start the process of trying to adhere to these "laws of respect." When you feel you are more aware and can correct this misstep most of the time, then repeat the process until you manage to cross everything off your list, Insha'Allah.

Chapter 19 – Intimacy

Unraveling the Taboo Topic of Intimate Relations

Despite being a practicing Muslim and trying hard to avoid this world's evils, the temptations of the dunya (world) are getting increasingly difficult and are a great trial. This is especially true in the Western world where society is heavily bombarded with sexual overtones and imagery such that its effects are almost impossible to avoid. Our world is riddled with lewdness and a lack of morality that it seeps into our day-to-day lives. Even if there is no television in the home, we still absorb its influence via the internet and today's fashion trends visible right from our front window. This onslaught of continuous sexually suggestive trends, behaviours, speech, and a deep level of shamelessness affects Muslim marriages everywhere! It would be naive for us as an ummah (nation) to turn a blind eye to it as it equally affects active, practising Muslim households.

With no real conversation to fall back onto, we grow up with subconscious expectations of what sexual intimacy should look and possibly feel like. However, there's an unnatural narrative presented and made to seem "normal" based on implicit behaviours we are exposed to in almost all movies, even children's movies. As well, our overall naivety allows us to accept these narratives as fact. Ultimately, there are many Muslim marriages suffering silently behind closed doors - disappointed and frustrated.

When the Devil's Plan Affects Us

Intimacy problems in a marriage aren't necessarily a lack of interest or effort, but they stem from a corrupt sense of what is real. Some couples that experience this overwhelmingly bitter pill in their marriage have developed their sense of reality based on the media, possibly their own sins, and/or the social depiction of what a healthy relationship looks like.

> "Shaytaan (Satan) made their deeds fair-seeming to them, and turned them away from the (Right) Path, though they were intelligent." *(Quran 29:38)*

It would be very ignorant on my part to assume that pornography, premarital, and extramarital relationships, even if non-sexual but still intimate, are not part of the Muslim struggle. Thus, I discuss them with openness, yet firmly assert that we should not accept any haram (forbidden) acts, even as "that's just how it is." Anything made forbidden for us is not the way of a believer.

One cannot undo what they see, as they cannot undo what they experience; they can only strive harder towards the way of righteousness and ask Allah for forgiveness, strength, and contentment.

Unfortunately, many Muslims engage in forbidden relationships and then decide to "settle down" and get married. Their family may pick a righteous, modest partner for them, as they may also want that for themselves. Sadly, while this is good to do, it's unrealistic to expect that just because you are married, you will be saved from temptations or that suddenly, because you are now married, you have freed yourself of the ills that had their grasp over you before marriage.

Shaytaan beautifies what is forbidden. Iblis' army is diligent in wanting us to continue in a state of rebelliousness and sin. Our carnal desires are a powerful source that can lead us away from Allah. Fortunately, Allah is most merciful and continuously forgiving. So, while we can repent and turn back to Allah, one must also understand that sins will affect us, and the consequences will result in some difficulty in our lives. In overcoming these adverse effects, patience (staying steadfast) is required. Despite not initially finding the same experiences as what haram actions may have temporarily given, eventually, one will find satisfaction in what is pure. The cleaner the heart becomes, the greater our ability to fully enjoy what is permissible.

The argument that only men are "tempted" towards haram is not true. Many women are in a similar situation wherein their past sins make it very difficult to find satisfaction in their halal marital relationship. This issue is not a gender issue. It's an issue of losing self-control and then trying to regain it while expecting that there will be no residual effects.

After acknowledging how merciful and forgiving Allah is, the first thing to know is that a God-conscious marriage is the devil's playing field. It is because these marriages are so sacred, he desperately seeks to corrupt them. Muslim marriages are a target for the shayateen, especially families working towards establishing the foundation of their home with Allah's remembrance. This harassment of the shayateen is unnecessary for those who are already sinning. Instead, Iblis' minions seek to destroy goodness and distract us from the remembrance of Allah by whispering suggestions. We have to accept this and become fully aware of it to protect ourselves as Shaytaan is an open enemy to us. His priority is to destroy the family structure.

> "O you who have believed, enter into Islam completely [and perfectly] and do not follow the footsteps of Satan. Indeed, he is to you a clear enemy." *(Quran 2:208)*

I will repeat this hadith since it's essential that we realize how vulnerable our marriages are if they are not protected.

The Messenger of Allah, peace and blessings be upon him, said, "Iblis places his throne upon water; he then sends detachments (for creating dissension); the nearer to him in rank are those who are most notorious in creating dissension. One of them comes and says: "I did so and so." And he says: "You have done nothing." Then one amongst them comes and says: "I did not spare so and so until I sowed the seed of discord between a husband and a wife." The Satan goes near him and says: "You have done well." A'mash said: He then embraces him."[45]

Whatever evils we may have experienced in our past and whatever society throws at us, Allah has given us the freedom to choose our own way right now (even if it's difficult). As well, He has not left us without protection. Reading the Quran, even without understanding it, is protection. Salah five times a day is also protection. Remembrance of Allah is also protection. Being in wudhu is also protection. Du'aa is also protection (refer to the last chapter for dua'as of protection). All these actions are for the sake of preserving ourselves in this world and the hereafter - Insha'Allah.

---

[45] Sahih Muslim 2813 b - Book 39, Hadith 6755

Sexuality and Gender

Sexual relations more often than not define the union of marriage and the health of a marriage. It is the difference between a friend and a marital relationship. It's an act that can bring unparalleled closeness and also hurt. It can be a means to great pleasure but also great humiliation. It simply depends on how it is approached.

Gender plays a significant role in how sexuality is perceived and understood. It's important to note the difference so that there isn't this constant need to blame the other gender for what they do or don't desire.

For a woman, she needs to experience emotional closeness: good conversations, cuddling, going out together, holding hands, compliments, possible gifts, and so on, to create a desire for sexual intimacy. For a man, his sexual desires are readily present. He battles with them constantly, and they are a great test and burden for him, especially so in today's society. For him, emotional closeness can only be explored once his sexual needs are fulfilled. Basically, "good sex leads to love" for men, and it's the opposite of that for women.

Leil Lowndes, the author of *How to Create Chemistry with Anyone*, sums it up quite simply: "A male wants sex first, then fondness, then love. A female wants fondness first, then love and sex together."

Obviously, this creates a very obvious problem. If a man needs sexual intimacy to be emotional, and a woman needs emotional closeness to be sexually interested, what does one do?

Islam answers this simply, as the right is given to the man, with the advice from our beloved Prophet, peace and blessings be upon him: "...Every game a Muslim plays is futile (Baatil) except for archery, training one's horse and playing with one's wife, for they are from praiseworthy acts."[46]

Therefore, a fair solution is for the wife to give-in lovingly to his desires and for the man to encourage her lovingly and seek to fulfill her needs too. There is so much beauty in this resolution.

While there is a level of awkwardness involved in this resolution since we typically act on our individual wants, it's essential to create a positive pattern of behaviour. This may take time, but once each

---

[46] Sunan Al-Tirmidhi 1637, Sunan Ibn Majah 2811 and Musnad Ahmad

understands the other and willingly accepts each other without manipulation, then security and comfort start to form.

It may look something like this: A husband seeks intimate relations with his wife, but his wife is not feeling emotionally connected (i.e., not in the mood), thus not seeking it, yet still returns her husband's approach lovingly and fulfills his needs. The husband understood his wife wasn't quite as interested as he was, so he slowed down to be extra gentle and loving (took patience and some restraint, but it paid off in the long run). The wife automatically felt closer to him, and slowly her desire became mutual. Therefore, both eventually enjoyed their time together, and the experience was mentally stored as a positive connection between the two. Both partners required a small level of sacrifice to accommodate the other. Both responded the way Islamic principles teach, and both reaped the reward of following these teachings: a woman responding to her husband and a man showing kindness. By Allah's mercy, this is not only rewarding on a tangible worldly level but also in the Hereafter!

Be Mindful of Each Other's Needs

Some spouses seem somewhat naive or utterly oblivious to how volatile a person becomes when their desires are not met. Sexual satisfaction is a strong indicator of a healthy marriage. Several studies have been done regarding marital satisfaction and sexual satisfaction. They concluded: "With the increase of sexual satisfaction, there was an increase in marital satisfaction"[47] or the reverse: with sexual dissatisfaction, there was an increase in marital problems.

Consider these scenarios.

Let's begin with the husband…

If a husband decides just to take his right, fulfill his desire and call it a day, it starts to create a compounded negative effect in the relationship. Eventually, it will become ingrained (programmed) in his wife's mind as a negative experience, which tends to result in his wife losing all desire. This internally creates hurt and humiliation for his

---

[47] Golestan University of Medical Sciences

wife, which results in her making conscious efforts to avoid the situation altogether.

The Prophet Muhammad, peace and blessings be upon him, said, "Do not begin intercourse until she has experienced desire like the desire you experience, lest you fulfill your desires before she does."[48]

In the case of the wife...

If a wife chooses to ignore (thus sinful) her husband's right and rejects his advances to initiate intimate relations, expect a few things to happen. He will become frustrated because the desire is there by no fault of his own, and a wife, equally serving as a garment to protect him from the outside temptations, is to be a means of respite for him (as he is to her). If she becomes unavailable over and over again, she's telling him she doesn't care about his needs. He will likely become passive-aggressive (or straight-up bitter) and find fault in other things that she does because of the resentment he has within. Eventually, he may start looking elsewhere, and if he brings up the topic of a second wife, know it's not because he doesn't love or desire his wife, but it's because every time he went to her, vulnerable with desire, she rejected him. To a man that says, "I don't love you," and eventually, he will respond to those unspoken words with what feels like the very same sentiments. While a second wife is a halal option, it may not necessarily be feasible. He may turn to pornography (that may or may not be an old habit that he was trying to ignore), or he may succumb to the women that choose to flirt and dress provocatively around him daily (in Western society).

It's not easy for him, and it would degrade the creation of Allah to ignorantly (and arrogantly) choose to refer to men as "dogs" - as some women like to do. His desire for sexual intimacy is a strong characteristic that Allah has made part of men, period. Of course, how he acts is a choice he makes, but know that a wife's role is to ease his burden and not make him feel cornered and desperate.

On the flip side... (yes, there is a flip side)

---

[48] Ibn Qudaamah Al-Maqdisi - Al Mughni 8:13

Today, many Muslim women complain about their husbands ignoring their sexual rights (thus sinful) and express frustration via social media groups. Naturally, some Muslim women are shy to ask concerning their desires, but according to the many forums online, even when she asks, he fails to comply. This would appear outside the nature of man. Unfortunately, it seems it is often due to the ill effects of pornography addiction (even those that fulfill their obligations in worship have been sucked into this immoral behaviour). Wives also complain that their husbands are on their phones, the computer or playing video games all night long, again, not making her right available and causing tension.

Husbands cannot expect that just because a woman does not have the same intensity of sexual desire as a man that she does not have it at all. Women, especially with the "love language" of physical touch (discussed in the next chapter), attribute sexual relations to feeling loved. Allah has made it mutually enjoyable for both spouses, and it is a right that cannot be neglected, especially in today's world.

Therefore, men need to be attentive to their wife's intimate needs, otherwise, she too can fall victim to the whispering of Shaytaan. Don't assume just because you take your wife for granted that there isn't another man, possibly even at her work (which is a reality for many working women), that desires her and is showing her more attention than you are. A man must be diligent in attending to his wife's needs just as she should be to his.

As for men and their complaints about women, rumour has it that they are bored in the bedroom. Muslims are exposed to many things, and while it's regrettable, it's still a struggle in dealing with it. Men are frustrated with the lack of spontaneity, attention, and the unexciting bedroom routine. I believe it's on the husband to suggest, nurture, and cultivate the excitement that he seeks, but while we're on the topic, wives can benefit from knowing that this is a common complaint among husbands. Wives, consider trying to express an openness to exploration, so he too does not feel shy or potentially judged by your reaction if he was to suggest something.

Deepening the Connection with Your Wife

There is no greater vulnerability to a modest, God-conscious Muslim woman than sexual intimacy. While Western society as a whole is promiscuous in nature, the practicing Muslim woman has guarded herself against falling prey to such immorality, even though it still influences her on some level.

For husbands, it is solely his responsibility to ensure the dynamics of sexual intimacy between each other feel safe, loving, and secure. This task can become hard work if his objective is only to satisfy his desires with the hopes that she'll go along and suddenly just love it. It won't happen, ever. By switching his mentality to ensure his wife feels safe, loved, and secure, he'll achieve wonderful things in the relationship.

Perhaps men might feel that placing this burden on them seems unjust because for him to feel love, stability, an emotional connection, and all the other positive relational emotions, sex is his starting point. I'm not suggesting the husband ignores his nature, but rather, inclusive of his nature, he also consistently remains attentive to his wife and not just when he has an end goal in mind for that day. Women know why and when their man suddenly notices her and is loving, randomly once or twice a week. Therefore, the goal is to make this level of attentiveness consistent, so she isn't able to recognize, "he's only nice because he wants something" (which makes her feel cheap and lowly).

Consider the following as pro-active steps for a husband to nurture the relational and intimate connection with his wife:

- If touch doesn't make her cringe, physically connect with her a few times during the day in a non-sexual manner. This builds security, grants attention, and nurtures a gradual physically intimate connection.

- Smile at her at least once a day. This creates love and shows a deep sense of admiration (sunnah too).

- Give her at least one genuine compliment. This breeds confidence in her, so when she's around you, she doesn't feel insecure but rather expresses a feel-good confidence.

- Help her with something that she often does without ever asking for your help: lift groceries, pick up toys, vacuum, clear the table, etc. This shows that you care, and her burden is yours (protectiveness).

The Bottom Line

Both husband and wife are Islamically bound to make a concentrated effort in fulfilling the sexual rights of each other. Both are equally entitled to the security, comfort, and attention that can only be found in each other. The times we live in are harsh. Thus, it would greatly benefit one's overall relationship if both husband and wife openly discuss their emotional and physical needs. It doesn't matter how long you have been married for, when the intimate relationship suffers, the rest of the marriage will too. It is the cornerstone of most marriages and foundational in creating a level of security and comfort.

Grow × Learn × Live

Work on creating positive patterns of behaviour. Nurture each other, and you'll soon see the fruits of your kindness, care, patience and consideration. If you cannot be open with one another, then who else can you be like that with? Enjoy what you have, without judgement.

GET HELP: There is no shame in seeking to rectify your actions. We are only given this lifetime to turn to Allah in repentance and to fix our problems. We are all sinful on different levels. While some actions create a greater sense of shame, you owe it to yourself, your soul, your akhira, and your family to work through those problems.

An ever-growing issue in the Muslim community is addiction to pornography. One cannot come to accept it as "that's just what happened to me." Set your intention to sincerely find a way out of this and Allah will make a way for you; through efforts and du'aa.

PurifyYourGaze.com specializes in dealing with Muslims that have sexual addictions. They have created a program to support and provide effective tools to understand and rid this habit. At the very least, start here. Don't allow shame to rob you of claiming back your life. Your mistakes do not define you, unless you allow them to, by simply not addressing them.

Chapter 20 – Love

What Is Love?

Love is a word used in many ways, shapes, and forms. It is greatly emphasized in the union of marriage to symbolize the level of closeness we have with our spouse. In the dictionary, in the noun form, it is defined as a "deep sense of affection for someone," and as a verb, it is defined as a "deep romantic or sexual attachment to someone."

While love describes an emotional state that manifests itself through specific actions, everyone has a different definition of what it is to them. It is seldom that both spouses perceive love the same way. Actions perceived as "love" are a combination of our experiences and personality.

For some people, it's considered loving when a spouse hugs them every time they come home. For another person, that's deemed to be overwhelming and possibly annoying. The way we perceive love is very important because, more often than not, that's also how we express love. Most couples are "loving" to one another, but because we interpret the meaning of love differently, the other person may simply not be able to see it. This is why we hear, "I've done everything I can, it's just never good enough!"

A successful marriage does not require an overwhelming amount of effort, to the point where it feels like a job. What it needs is the right type of effort that produces positive results.

Of course, the next question is, "Well, what is the right type of effort?" The answer first requires individual thought because many of us are oblivious to our own selves.

Start by completing this sentence:

I feel *most* loved (or happy) when . . .

Both partners should answer this question: write down your answer and share it with each other. It is the most valuable piece of information that you will have regarding each other. By knowing their perspective of love, you can successfully (and confidently) approach tough conversations, express how much they mean to you and establish your commitment to one another in a manner that is understood. The catch here - ensure the reply to the above question is the absolute truth!

In the very well-known book by Gary Chapman, *The 5 Love Languages*, he speaks about how we all receive love differently. He has broken this down into five key categories that he refers to it as, "love languages." Our love language is understood through actions, words, and gestures, that are all done without any personal agenda, just the other person's pleasure.

Typically, one or two of these "love languages" will dominate how we receive love or when we feel loved. This doesn't mean we don't like or enjoy what is suggested in the other categories, but when we experience one or two of these categories, we feel very blessed and fortunate for our significant other. The acts that make us want to randomly tell our spouse "I love you" or "You're the best!" or "I feel so blessed to have you in my life!" are deeply infused in our perception of love and our ability to receive those gestures as "love."

Reflect on the following five categories and see which actions make you feel good when your spouse does them for you. Also, take notice of the things you do that makes your spouse feel chipper and upbeat.

Love Language	What It Is	Expressed By
Words of Affirmation	Honest verbal compliments (not flattery). Appreciative, encouraging, humble and kind words.	"I feel blessed to be married to you," "You're a great friend," "You have the best ideas" etc.
Quality Time	Spending time together by being mentally present and genuinely interested. Getting focused, undivided attention from the person you are with.	Quality conversations that make you feel heard and understood, doing quality activities together to experience something together. Enjoying time together.
Receiving Gifts	A visual symbol of someone's love. The physical manifestation of someone's knowledge of you (what you like, want, fear, don't like, etc.) and their thoughts about you, sometimes even their presence ("gift of self").	Expressed by a spontaneous gift that shows attentiveness to your words: buying your favourite food, buying the type of socks you had said you love, etc. Being by your side in your time of joy or need, especially when you know they'd rather be elsewhere.
Acts of Service	The things you find important or want help with that are done for you, in a positive, kind manner. Receiving a helping hand in the tasks you are faced with.	Often expressed in day-to-day activities that your spouse knows you'd like their help with: vacuuming, children's homework, grocery shopping, cleaning the bathroom, etc.
Physical Touch	To be physically touched by your spouse in a manner which *you* find comfort in; otherwise, it may be deemed irritating. Not to be mistaken with strong sexual needs. Feeling the need for random, non-sexual touch.	Expressed through your spouse's unprompted gestures to physically connect, such as hugs, holding hands, touch on the shoulder, massage, etc.

The Universal Show of Love

It's interesting to note Gary Chapman's comments regarding gift giving: "I examined the cultural patterns surrounding love and marriage and found that in every culture I studied, gift giving was a part of the love marriage process." He expressed how it has profound practical implications for couples and may even transcend cultural barriers.

Of course, it's not surprising to find this in the sunnah of our beloved Prophet Muhammad, peace and blessings be upon him. He used to send gifts to the family of Khadijah, may Allah be pleased with her, as a show of his deep love for her. People would also do the same for him, by gifting him land, food, and their services as an expression of their love for him, upon whom be peace and blessings.

The sacred advice is as follows:

The Prophet, peace and blessings be upon him, said, "Give each other gifts and you will love each other."[49]

Not only are we encouraged to give gifts, but the validity of a marriage in Islam includes the dowry, which is not considered a gift in shar'iah but in its own way plays that role. This simple act of honouring one's bride builds a special love at a time a woman would feel most vulnerable. This act also dignifies a woman's position by giving her this God-given right of receiving a dowry which she also has the right to choose; and only with it, is her marriage valid before Allah!

The Messenger of Allah, peace and blessings be upon him, said: "Any woman whose marriage is not arranged by her guardian, her marriage is invalid, her marriage is invalid, her marriage is invalid. If (the man) has had intercourse with her, then the mahr (dowry) belongs to her in return for his intimacy with her. And if there is any dispute then the ruler is the guardian of the one who does not have a guardian."[50]

---

[49] Al-Adab Al-Mufrad 594 - Bukhari
[50] Sunan Ibn Majah - Book 9, Hadith 35 - Vol. 3, Book 9, Hadith 1879

Figuring Out Your Spouse's Love Language(s)

While we may know our spouses well, it's not actually that obvious what their love language is (or ours, for that matter). So, consider asking your spouse what their love language(s) is, and if that doesn't get you far, think about this: What does your spouse do when they know you're upset? I'm not talking about a full-blown fight, but when tension starts rising. What do they do when things are still pretty good between you both, but there's an air of conflict looming? How do they try to ease the situation?

Typically, their response will indicate what they consider to be loving or, in some cases, what they choose to withhold. Even if they verbally respond to any potential issue, they likely might also be doing something else. They may choose to clean (acts of service) or pick-up some dessert that night (gift giving). Perhaps they may say something sweet or compliment you (words of affirmation). Maybe they'll put their distractions away and start up a conversation (quality time). Perhaps if they know you're not too happy, they'll keep hovering around you in your personal space bubble while finding excuses to touch you (physical touch). Whatever way they react is an indication of their perception of love. Unless, of course, they've figured you out and know what you like. In which case, you'll have to do some more digging.

Noticing how you react is also a good way to figure your own love language, if you haven't managed to do it already.

If you don't have the same love language (this often is the case), you can perceive their actions as annoying, manipulative, etc. In reality, they are merely trying to be as loving as possible. This is them making an effort.

How you express your love to someone is usually how you perceive it. Though this is not always the case, you'll often find your individual beliefs of love manifest in the way you treat others.

Grow × Learn × Live

You might not know what your "love language" is right away, but a good way of figuring it out would be by asking, "What does an ideal day with my spouse look like?" When you can paint the picture of a great day with your spouse, you'll be able to see how you best feel loved. Share it with your spouse. It works best when you can both gain perspective on each other.

When you have a good sense of how your partner perceives love, then don't delay in doing those things. It will take some time for them to see consistency in your actions, but when they do, you'll likely notice your relationship getting stronger, Insha'Allah!

Chapter 21 – The Way to a Woman's Heart *(Advice to Men)*

Understanding Her Needs

Are women as complex as they seem? Absolutely! While nothing is entirely black and white or across the board with us women, there are some fundamentals that can be applied when interacting with one's wife.

The author of *Men Are From Mars, Women Are From Venus*, Dr. John Gray says, "Women primarily need caring, understanding, respect, devotion, validation, and reassurance."

APPRECIATION

Husbands like to ask their wives: "What do you want? What will make you happy?"

In the book, *How to Win Friends & Influence People,* the author Dale Carnegie quotes a man named James William who says, "the greatest principle of human nature is to feel appreciated." This is not limited to gender, but it is especially true for women as their work often goes unrewarded and unnoticed. This advice is foundational in winning the heart of your wife by not taking her love, efforts, and sacrifices for granted (even if she might do that to you).

Acknowledge what she does by verbalizing it since women respond stronger and faster if you verbally communicate your appreciation. This saves her having to "figure it out" or to try to see the good in the attempts you make to "show" her your appreciation (an expression of one's love).

Appreciating your wife requires you to show care, validation and offer reassurance in noticing what she does. This has to be done for her to feel good, though it may not necessarily make you feel warm and fuzzy inside when you do it, since it's not a pressing need for you.

ATTENTION

Most women deeply desire attention on some level. Not all attention is equally measured, so the success of this effort would depend entirely on the personality of your woman. Possible ways of fulfilling this need might be: making her feel fully visible to you and that you value her in your life. Try to be explicit in showing her attention, otherwise, she may miss it.

In showering your wife with your attentiveness, you're expressing your devotion to her. Similarly, you may watch a game for 3 hours and value the time you spent doing it, a wife wishes for such sentiments. She desires rest and relaxation be in her company, but not in her company with UFC on, instead being interested in who she is, what she's doing, how she's feeling and of course, how she's looking. Attention tells your wife, she's special to you, and that's all that matters to her.

Without your attention, she feels unimportant, neglected, unloved, and possibly unworthy. Over time, she'll likely seek out other company that fulfills this need, but then don't be surprised if you're not at the top of her list anymore.

SECURITY

Women are very loyal by nature (generally speaking); this is why it is so hard for many women to understand polygyny from a male perspective. Women are jealous, yes, but not to the extent a man holds onto jealousy. A woman's jealousy comes from her loyalty to her husband. She can't truly love more than one man, so she cannot fathom how he will view her with the same devotion, love, and affection if he had another wife in his life.

A husband must understand a woman's top priority is to feel secure. Security for her means she isn't worried that her needs won't be met, such as the need for attention, the need for protection either as emotional or physical support, her need for financial resources in providing food, shelter, recreation for her and the children, etc. Even if she works, she still has these needs from you, her husband. While it may feel like a full-time job, once a system that satisfies both your needs is firmly established, things will run with ease, Insha'Allah. Ensuring that you create a sense of emotional, financial, and physical security for your wife offers her reassurance. Of course, things will come up, and it's not always so simple to do, but being mindful of this need for security will help alleviate a lot of her fear-based triggers.

LISTEN & TALK WITH HER

Women like to talk and want to be heard, some more than others, but this is the general nature of women. It's a need of a woman to feel understood, and through that, her emotional and mental position is validated.

While some men don't particularly like talking, they need to learn to give their wives a reason to stay mentally engaged with them (just as much as she has to for him).

It's interesting to note what Dr. John Gray, an expert in gender differences, has said regarding this: "After the Martians (men) learned how to listen, they made a most amazing discovery. They began to realize that listening to a Venusian (women) talk about problems could actually help them come out of their caves in the same way as watching the news on TV or reading a newspaper. Similarly, as men learn to listen without feeling blamed or responsible, listening becomes much easier. As a man gets good at listening, he realizes that listening can be an excellent way to forget the problems of his day as well as bring a lot of fulfillment to his partner."

Every woman is different, so deciding how much listening is necessary or what to talk about will depend entirely on the woman you're married to. Of course, this shouldn't be a chore, or at least the attitude behind your presence should not be negative. Nonetheless, try to make conversation, engage her mind, learn about each other. She'll feel like you care about who she is (and hopefully you do!), and you can bridge any gaps that have formed in your relationship.

Choose to Show Up

Consistency in expressing your commitment to your marriage is important for women; this also falls under the need for reassurance and validation.

Perhaps men don't find much benefit or even a need in expressing their commitment since, "I'm here, aren't I?" is the general attitude. But for women, this is important because, to her, it validates her worth in your eyes. Try to commit to habits that nurture and appreciate. Stick to them daily as these will set a positive tone in your marriage. By doing this, you're telling her that she matters all the time and not only when you need something from her. Over time, when you consistently keep showing up, the need for reassurance will be less - you'll both know when that security sets in your marriage, it's when you find peace and comfort in each other. It doesn't take much. Believe it or not, the little things go a long way.

On special days, when you're feeling good and feeling confident, try doing something different, just for her: stop at the store just to get her favourite snack, get her an outfit you think she'll look gorgeous in (and tell her that too), pick up dinner and let her know you want her to take it easy, take her out for a drive around town and maybe tell her you miss spending time together, bring home some flowers and tell her it reminded you of her etc. It can even be as little as randomly saying "I love you" for no apparent reason. Refer to her "love language" in the previous chapter (chapter 20) for optimal results.

A key in doing that extra something is that the delivery of this gesture is essential. This is why with each suggestion I followed it up with another suggestion for the delivery. What you say when you do something extra is where the "magic" happens! If you bring flowers and throw them on the table, it'll mean nothing. If you get food, grab a plate and eat without asking about her or anyone else – again, it's pointless. It might even cause conflict if attached to the gesture is a stink or selfish attitude.

Every once in a while, change things up based on what you would mutually enjoy. This works as a breath of fresh air in your marriage when it's done lovingly.

Neglect Can Be Heartbreaking

Men make the mistake of thinking, "She will never leave," but when a woman is worn out and neglected, don't assume your children or your history together is enough to keep her in your life. Even if she doesn't complain about your constant distraction with sports, friends, continuously doing things without family, living as though you're in a hotel, etc., don't assume she's not hurting. While women are typically very loyal, that too can have an expiration date. It is often an unexpected one, especially when she feels there is no one around for her to be loyal to.

So, husbands, don't become lackadaisical in your marriage. Refer to your wife's "love language" to know the right effort required to kindle her respect, feelings of safety, and her overall emotional connection with you.

Note: Many men like to stay "comfortable" and not make an extra effort beyond what comes naturally to them. They may even exert themselves tremendously in that way, but if that's not how their wife perceives love, they're pretty much doing that to make themselves feel good. Sometimes, or most times, we have to get a little uncomfortable and do what might feel a bit awkward at first, for the sake of building that connection.

Remember, you're doing it to make her happy, not you. It doesn't take much, but it does require an effort. Even if she's not asking you to show up at all in her life, it doesn't mean she doesn't desire it. She likely has some insecurity in herself or the relationship developed in such a way that it prevents her from expressing her emotional needs to you.

Support

We don't live in a time where women are limited to one avenue in life. Despite choosing to be a wife and possibly gifted the role of being a mother, many women have other aspirations. In a time where opportunities are endless in the exploration of interests, it is unrealistic to expect that your wife will limit herself to a set role, especially as your children get older.

Being open to whatever ideas she might have or see for herself is important for a healthy relationship (as you'd like her to do for you). Even if some of her ideas aren't quite what you agree with, don't begin any dialogue by shooting her ideas down. Listen with an attentive ear.

Some men consider a woman's aspirations as a threat to their manhood, but they aren't. Not all women choose to kill time by cooking, cleaning, and quietly scrolling through Facebook. Some love it, but not all do. It's a matter of preference, so try to be open to it. Of course, always set the foundation of such conversations by grounding them in Islamic guidelines and make that the boundary of exploration.

Support for a woman isn't only limited to her aspirations. Sometimes it's just a shoulder to lean on. That doesn't mean you have to start mimicking how her girlfriends offer her emotional support, but you can be there for her as her man - as her husband. That might just look like an arm around her when you can see she's emotionally worn out, or a word of appreciation, or even a du'aa (supplication) for her ease. These are simple but intimate ways to show your support for her specifically.

Yes, specifically. Think about it. Who buys customized products with names on them or something sentimental on them? Women. Specifics matter to women, including the nicknames you have given her (or haven't given). It's hard for men to see this because men focus on the overall picture and don't care about details or what appears to be sentimental. One or two "specifics" is all it takes. No one is suggesting you become someone different, but a little extra effort speaks volumes.

A Word of Caution

There is a common habit among men that rubs many women the wrong way and makes everything seem ugly to them. Therefore, being mindful about it might make all the difference for you.

While it is understood that sexual intimacy is a stronger need for men, a man cannot overlook his wife's need for emotional security to complement his needs. Too many men only decide to appreciate their wives close to the evening, or if they are away, take extra care to check in on them only when they are returning, etc. The point is, her man is only attentive when he wants something (…yes, she knows it very well). We all have patterns of behaviour. If your pattern of behaviour is only to act lovingly when you want something, then obviously you're creating a negative dynamic in the relationship. Just like if your wife only approaches you for intimacy because she wants money to make a big purchase, you're not going to enjoy the experience as much as when you know she desires closeness to you. You'd likely go through it all, accept it, but it still has an ugly vibe lingering.

Be sincere in showing affection to your wife. Do it for her and not just for your desire(s) to be fulfilled. The reality is that if you do things to nourish the relationship, then the fulfillment of your desires will be a natural process. In fact, it'll likely be sweeter since it would have been mutually sought after and enjoyed.

It's On You

Here's the honest truth - if you aren't fulfilled in the bedroom, then brothers, it's on you! I've said this in earlier chapters, but just in case you missed it, here's an analogy to bring it home.

Consider this a bit like sales. Why would she pay top dollar for cheap China goods? High ticket sales are sold by creating the ambiance required to suit the targeted clientele. That means, for you to expect your wife to do more than fulfill rights (because she isn't obligated to pretend to enjoy it or want to be there), then you have to make an irresistible offer. If you don't want to take the time to do that, don't expect more than what you're putting in (...*just saying*).

Balance

Lastly, remember not to overdo it.

Your goal is to nurture your relationship; it's not for you to assume your wife's responsibilities or role. You are the man of the house, and by taking charge in nurturing aspects of the relationship, you also boost your confidence. Nonetheless, the idea is not to follow her lead but to show up. Be there in support of her, especially when she does not expect it. Aim to do this daily because a mindful woman deeply appreciates it and, arguably, needs the reminder.

Grow × Learn × Live

This building block is quite specific because it includes simple gestures that can be done consistently. By keeping things easy and knowing what it takes, the likelihood of you doing it is much higher. Consider the following and start nurturing those good vibes!

- Non-sexual touch (at least two times a day)
- Smile (at least once a day)
- Genuine compliment (at least once a day)
- Help her with something (at least once a day)

Chapter 22 – The Way to a Man's Heart *(Advice to Women)*

Understanding His Needs

Men aren't like us, women. They are much simpler. We, women, often confuse men with our complexities because, understandably, we simply can't relate. The simplicity of a man does not mean that he is incapable of loving hard. It just means he loves differently. Part of enjoying a place in your man's heart is understanding that he is not like you. He won't show love the way you do, and he doesn't feel or react the way you do, but that doesn't mean he doesn't love you as much as you love him.

The rebuttal to this is, "But if I can do it, he can too!" - right? Not necessarily. Despite both being human, we are still wired differently, with a different set of hormones, a different set of needs, different perceptions, etc.

"When we expect our partners to be more like us, we are automatically giving them the message that they are not good enough the way they are."[51]

The author of *Men Are From Mars, Women Are From Venus,* Dr. John Gray, writes about men's needs: "Men primarily need trust, acceptance, appreciation, admiration, approval, and encouragement." As well, Steve Harvey, the author of *Act Like a Women, Think Like a Man* sums up a man's needs in his book with three defining characteristics: "loyalty, support, and the cookie (sex)." Much of what Dr. Gray says can be found in a woman's expression of loyalty and support.

"Real romance occurs when we are able to nurture our partner's needs."[52]

LOYALTY

A woman's loyalty to her man is a very tender concept to him because she resolves to stand by her husband even when she doesn't

---

[51] Dr. John Gray - *Men Are From Mars, Women Are From Venus*
[52] Dr. John Gray - *Men Are From Mars, Women Are From Venus*

quite understand his logic or there is hardship and uncertainty that even he feels anxious about.

In a woman's loyalty, she is expressing that she trusts, approves and accepts her husband. Consequently, this works as motivation for him to be a better man. It also means the world to him. However, if a wife chooses to criticize and compare her husband, her loyalty becomes blurred, and he will feel abandoned.

This type of loyalty is very apparent in the relationship between the Prophet, peace and blessings be upon him, and his beloved wife Khadijah, may Allah be pleased with her. Khadijah, may Allah be pleased with her, came from affluence and a social circle comprised of the elite of the time, with many that had shunned her husband - peace and blessings be upon him. Yet this magnificent woman, one who reached perfection, stood firmly by her husband with an unwavering belief in him and his ability to fulfill the great task upon him. She also willingly endured the boycott placed on the tribe of the Prophet, peace and blessings be upon him, which did not include her. Yet, she chose hardship so she could be by his side and care for him. This demonstrates the essence of loyalty. It requires great trust, respect, and ultimately self-sacrifice.

In a woman's loyalty, she wants her husband to be a better version of himself. However, that cannot be achieved by pointing out his past errors or weaknesses. She has to do it by emphasizing his amazing qualities, thus giving him the confidence to soar to his greatest, Insha'Allah.

Another more commonly understood aspect of loyalty is that of a woman's direct (wife) relationship with her husband. This loyalty is found in her virtue and desire for none but her husband; a characteristic of the promised wives of Jannah. If that is a promised Jannati reward to a man, it speaks volumes about how important it is to him! A man deeply desires his wife to be committed to him only: physically, emotionally, and mentally (arguably more than a woman wants to have him to herself).

Naturally, as believing women, our loyalty to our husband has one condition - that it does not contradict anything in the Quran or Sunnah.

This submissive nature is challenging in a Western society that celebrates the "independent woman" mindset and declares feministic views as the ultimate success while shunning anything counter to it. In reflecting on the ideology of feminism, one can see that it isn't in women's best interest.

Women's rights have long been afforded to us through Islamic law, in perfect measure, even if there are Muslim men who choose to ignore those rights. Feminism actually strips away a woman's essence, forcing her to change her nature to what is now considered "right," and everything else is wrong.

It is interesting to see an emerging countermovement by Western women called "Tradewifehood" or "Tradewives" that advocates feminine self-improvement. A supporter of this trending perspective said, "I simply think the old ways were better: when men provided and protected, and women took care of their men. I just ask not to be judged." Unfortunately, the feminist movement has been so overwhelming and dominant that women fear judgement by merely wanting to be a wife and enjoy motherhood.

Ultimately though, even as Muslim women, we can choose. But in choosing, it would be wise to weigh the demands of feminism and the risks of overstepping the boundaries set for the believer, against the rights Muslim women are blessed with, through comprehensive Islamic laws.

The Messenger of Allah, peace and blessings be upon him, said, "If a woman prays her five prayers, fasts her month of Ramadan, guards her chastity, and obeys her husband, she will enter Paradise from any gate she wishes."[53]

With the reward of Jannah, what more is left to be desired?

SUPPORT

Support to a man is listening to his dreams and aspirations without giving him reasons not to do it. This falls under a man's need for encouragement and appreciation.

When the Prophet Muhammad, peace and blessing be upon him, first encountered angel Jibril, he thought he was losing his mind and rushed to the one he knew with absolute certainty had his back, his

---

[53] Ṣaḥīḥ Ibn Ḥibban 4252

wife Khadijah, may Allah be pleased with her. She reminded him of his good traits and comforted him when he was filled with self-doubt. Similarly, using words of encouragement and reminding your husband of all the reasons he can do something (even if it scares you a bit) is a need he has. It empowers him and thus empowers your relationship.

Supporting your husband is not something that should be taken lightly. Simply because you bore him children does not mean that you believe in him. You have to verbalize it and manifest it through encouraging words and positivity.

The Prophet, peace and blessings be upon him, said about his beloved wife Khadijah, may Allah be pleased with her: "She believed in me while the people disbelieved in me. And she trusted in me while the people belied me. And she helped and comforted me in person and in wealth when the people would not. Allah provided me with children by her, and He did not with others."[54]

Part of showing support to a man is also being grateful for the things that he does. Many times, we can overlook the good actions our husband does for us: possibly out of anger, feelings of neglect or our own weaknesses. Nonetheless, a powerful reminder has been given to us women by way of our beloved Prophet, peace and blessings be upon him, such that we must be very diligent in ensuring we do not become ungrateful to our husband.

The Prophet, peace and blessings upon him, said: "I was shown the Hellfire and that the majority of its dwellers were women who were ungrateful." It was asked, "Do they disbelieve in Allah?" (or are they ungrateful to Allah?) He replied, "They are ungrateful to their husbands and are ungrateful for the favors and the good (charitable deeds) done to them. If you have always been good (benevolent) to one of them and then she sees something in you (not of her liking), she will say, 'I have never received any good from you.'"[55]

---

[54] Musnad Imam Ahmad 6/118
[55] Sahih al-Bukhari 29 - Book 2, Hadith 22

A woman's role of support means, through the expression of gratitude, she creates emotional safety for her husband to let his guard down. Steve Harvey says, "…appreciating a man; not undermining his confidence, is the best way to get the best out of your guy. And the best way to appreciate him is by being a girl, and especially letting him be a man."

Also, there are women that like to "joke" that their husband is like an extra child, yet they fail to realize he has needs just as much as she does. In wanting a beautiful marriage, we have to understand that for men to give us their all, they have to do it based on their own nature and not our demands.

A controlling wife is unanimously the most unattractive quality for a man. Such action is often steeped in ingratitude. Her attempt to control him works to strip him of his manhood, thus most husbands will resist doing such demands even if he wanted to do it. He may even become passive aggressive (i.e., mean) or do the opposite, simply to reassert his self-worth. "Taking control of a situation" is not supportive, no matter how it is packaged to look.

Treat a man like a man, and he'll respond like one. Try to control a man and strip him of his authority, manhood, and protective-providing-nature, then you'll see the "child" that women often complain about.

Only After 'Needs' Are There 'Wants'

"THE COOKIE"

To understand a man without being offended by his nature, we have to realize that a man can easily fulfill his sexual desires without actually feeling close to the person he is with, unlike most women. It can easily be a simple act to satisfy carnal desires, period—nothing more, nothing less. Yet, with the right mindset of both husband and wife, it can open the door to a much deeper relationship.

A man's sexual needs are his number one priority in marriage because the desire is naturally present, and obviously, he can only fulfill that in a halal way with his wife. He needs a safe, fun, cooperative outlet to express that. When a wife learns to respect that this is how Allah created men, and she honours this by being available to her husband's needs, he will instinctively begin the process of emotional closeness. This is because he begins to feel secure in the marriage. Accepting a man's needs without question is a manifestation of respect, which is also a need that men have; to be respected.

Social stigmas like to depict men as insensitive and emotionless creatures, which is entirely false. Men are no different from women in many ways - they also feel insecure, emotionally needy, and are also scared in the relationship. They desire an intimate, emotional connection, but their physical needs come first. Humans are such that our basic needs pull at us, and only after we fulfill them, do we have the mental space to develop wants that go beyond simply satisfying the necessities.

That said, many times, women hold onto these stigmas without giving their husbands a chance to create that emotional connection. By actually listening to what he is saying and not judging his words based on one's own interpretation (i.e., he's just saying that because he wants sex, he's just nice because I do so much and he can't live without me, he's just complaining because he doesn't want to take responsibility, etc.), true intimacy can be created in the relationship.

You Are His Protection

Wives have a vital role in protecting their husbands from the outside world. He sees too much even by merely leaving the house to go to the masjid. He hears too much just by leaving the house to do the grocery shopping. His senses are overwhelmed, and you are his God-given gift to settle all the turmoil within.

Allah's Messenger, peace and blessings be upon him, saw a woman and so he came to his wife, Zainab, may Allah be pleased with her, as she was tanning a leather and had sexual intercourse with her. He then went to his companions and told them: "The woman advances and retires in the shape of a devil, so when one of you sees a woman, he should come to his wife, for that will repel what he feels in his heart."[56]

---

[56] Sahih Muslim 1403a - Book 8, Hadith 3240

Develop a habit of approaching your husband with compassion and an understanding so that you can serve an even greater purpose in your marriage than you think. As his wife, you are gifted with the traits that can mentally, physically, and emotionally centre your husband's being unlike anything else.

A protection – the characteristic of a garment. It's your choice alone which type of garment you wish you to be.

You Are His Comfort

Your husband cannot function without you, even if you drive him insane. It is only through you that the necessary stability for your husband can be established.

Your husband's needs are greatly limited compared to yours. And no, he doesn't love you just for sex, but he needs sex to love you. Understand this well. Again, he doesn't love you because of sex (he can do it and feel nothing towards you), but to love you, he needs that sexual connection with you. Desire and love are two different emotions to a man. His desires can have no emotional connection, and they can be triggered by any woman, possibly even a billboard *(don't quote me on this)*.

Men want their wives to enjoy physical intimacy as much as they do. They feel more pleasure (due to emotional connectedness) when their wife is just as enthusiastic. Your enthusiasm tells him that he can be emotionally vulnerable with you, that he doesn't have to hide his desires or feel shame for them with you. It tells him that you accept him, thus igniting his own interest to deeply know and accept you too. Ultimately, it tells him that you genuinely care about him and when he knows that with certainty, he opens the door to his thoughts, feelings, and true nature.

While women tend to be shy in terms of sexual intimacy, it's not necessary for you to throw yourself at him for him to feel the above-mentioned. Men notice a lot more than they like to show. They just don't like talking about what they notice (unlike women). Your openness to him will be apparent just in your demeanour. Keep in mind that men, too, can often feel equally vulnerable and insecure in respect to sexual intimacy, and it's up to his woman to build his confidence. There's no better way to do that than showing him your interest in him.

Research was done to see what attracted men to approach a woman. Naturally, it was expected that beauty was the incentive they needed to muster up the courage to approach a woman. It turned out that was not it: "If you are friendly and obviously flirtatious, men are more apt to approach you than they are the most gorgeous woman in the room."[57] The allure is in the attitude!

I encourage every woman to commit to the list below with the intention to love your husband on his terms and be a source of security for him - ultimately for the pleasure of Allah.

- At least once a day, be playful with your husband: blow a kiss, wink, hug him from behind (so it's not expected he return the gesture), say something sweet, find something to laugh about, etc.

- At least once a week, take 20 minutes and make yourself look good. You have to be able to look in the mirror and say, "MashaAllah, lookin' good girl!" Don't worry if the house is a mess. Just make sure you're on point. A little is a lot for a man, so don't feel you need celebrity makeup and expensive clothes – he doesn't care, but he'll appreciate you're doing it for him. Men are visual creatures and thoroughly enjoy seeing their woman looking her best!

- Every day for at least 10 minutes, sit next to your husband or across (don't be walking around) and listen to him talk about anything other than you and the children. It might take an effort to get him to talk, so ask questions. Show an interest in him as a man. Don't worry about being awkward or weird. Just pay him your undivided attention – your children will be fine.

- At least once a day, serve him like a king. Ask if you can get him something, make him his favourite cookies and take them to him, grab him a cushion so he can sit back and relax, make

---

[57] Leil Lowndes – *How to Create Chemistry with Anyone*

him a cup of tea, etc. Do this with a loving, positive attitude. If you're crusty and basically behaving like you hate him, then you're not going to achieve much good (or any at all!). This effort is a show of respect, an inherently strong need a man has.
- At least once a day, thank him for something he has done for you (and the family).

With everything, be sure to do it in moderation. Balance is key! Doing too much will change the dynamics in the male-female relationship and relay the message that "you don't need a man." A man needs to be needed but loves positive attention from his woman (and who wouldn't!).

Also, by doing too much, you're not helping him to perceive, recognize, or attend to your needs. Men need motivation, so keep things balanced otherwise he might wrongly assume he need not do anything because "things are just great!"

Note: It's important to point out that while intimacy is a more substantial need for a man, it does not mean he has this need 24/7. Bear in mind, men too can "not be in the mood," and just because he isn't, it does not mean he finds his wife unattractive, doesn't love her, or worse, is cheating on her. He may be tired, may have a lot on his mind, etc. He too, needs the space to be himself. Of course, if a woman is continually making an effort and her advances are turned down each time, an open discussion about it needs to be had. Not only is it the right of the wife too, but without open communication, this form of rejection can have profound negative effects on the marriage and lead to a lot of passive-aggressive behaviour (on both sides).

... Just the Way You Are

A lack of confidence in one's physical self makes enjoying intimacy difficult. You have to trust that your husband is attracted to you regardless of how you see yourself. If, for whatever reason, you don't believe that Allah has created all His creations with beauty (including you), then you need to ask yourself if you have the right to even feel that way.

Every creation of Allah's is beautiful, and everyone will see beauty differently. Beautify yourself with clothes that make you feel good, with a modest amount of makeup that will enhance your natural features and not cover them like a mask of insecurity. Husbands find it super annoying how their woman complains about her looks (and weight). It's actually insulting to his taste and works to diminish the pride he feels when he sees you.

Putting yourself down suggests that your husband could have done better (for lack of a better term); again it's insulting to him. So, don't project negativity or self-sabotage by trying to convince him that he doesn't see your beauty just because you can't. Take time to yourself to look good, so you'll feel good. It'll be contagious! Plus, he'll be super excited that he landed such a fine catch! (Masha'Allah).

Abusing Your Power

Sexual intimacy should not be used as a punishment (i.e., withholding it because you are angry or don't get what you want). Doing this is the fastest way for your husband to block you out of his happy thoughts. It breeds deep resentment (just as it breeds resentment from a woman when a man is only sweet and loving when he wants something).

Consider intimate relations as your husband's medicine. Even if you think he's an idiot that week, he still needs to take his medication, so he doesn't become ill (i.e., more of an idiot). It is a deep need he has. It's halal, you are rewarded for it, you are the only one he can lawfully enjoy it with in the entire world, and it keeps him balanced. Make it a priority in your marriage and not an afterthought if you "feel" like it, or worse, feel "he deserves it." He's your garment, and you are his.

Does He Love You?

In the same book, *Act Like a Women, Think Like a Man*, Steve Harvey offers insight into the behaviours and mindset of men. He says to know if a man loves you, he will do three things: "profess, provide and protect."

Profess means he won't hide who you are to him. You are his woman, and he'll make sure everyone knows it, "Back off, she's taken!"

"Protect" means he is defensive about you - your physical and emotional well-being (he truly tries to help even if he doesn't get it right).

Lastly, to provide is a characteristic mentioned in the Quran and hadith regarding the role of a man. A man feels valuable, loved, and honoured when he can provide for his family, even if it requires him to do more work. When a man is attached and loves his woman, he will ensure he fulfills her tangible needs to the best of his ability.

> "Men are the protectors and maintainers of women, because Allah has made one of them to excel the other and because they spend (to support them) from their means. Therefore, the righteous women are devoutly obedient (to Allah and to their husbands) and guard, in the husband's absence, what Allah orders them to guard (i.e. their chastity, their husband's property, etc.) ..." *(Quran 4:34)*

Interestingly, the first two characteristics, profess and protect, are often misunderstood in today's world as a "jealous man" since this concept stems from feminist views. Modern times consider these characteristics as unfavourable and "backwards." Nonetheless, men in their most authentic selves are more jealously protective of their woman than a woman is over her man. He just shows it differently. When a man is "jealous" over his woman, he is professing and protecting - characteristics very much a part of a manly man.

The Prophet, peace and blessings be upon him, said, "Three people will not enter paradise, and Allah will not look to them on the Day of Judgement: the one who is disobedient to his parents, the woman who imitates men, and the Dayooth."[58]

Ibn Al-Qayyim, may Allah have mercy on him, said, "And the dayooth (the man with no jealousy over the woman and his family)

---

[58] Musnad Ahmad

is the most vile of Allah's creation, and Jannah is forbidden for him (because of his lack of ghirah-jealousy)."

Definition: Protective Jealousy (Ghirah)

Ghirah: This Arabic word covers a broad meaning – self-respect, jealousy (with regards to women) – and it is a feeling of fury with great anger when one's honour and prestige is challenged or injured.

Sa`d bin Ubada said, "If I found a man with my wife, I would kill him with the sharp side of my sword." When the Prophet, peace and blessings be upon him, heard what he said, "Do you wonder at Sa`d's sense of ghirah (self-respect)? Verily, I have more sense of ghirah than Sa`d, and Allah has more sense of ghirah than I."[59]

Men Need Space

Men are often criticized by their women for not being present, for not listening, or for being reclusive. True, it seems they tend to have bad timing when they need that space (such as after intimate relations, a common complaint women have), but still, they need it. It's not because of you. A man's need for space is simply how his brain is wired; some need it more than others. Men need mental space and time alone to take in everything they're feeling and figure it out, especially when they are stressed in some way.

Gender relations guru, Dr. John Gray says, "When a man is stressed, he will withdraw into the cave of his mind and focus on solving a problem. At such times, he becomes increasingly distant, forgetful, unresponsive, and preoccupied in his relationships. At such times he is incapable of giving a woman the attention and feeling that she normally receives and certainly deserves. His mind is preoccupied, and he is powerless to release it. If, however, he can find a solution, instantly he will feel much better and come out of his cave; suddenly he is available for being in a relationship again. If he cannot find a solution to his problem, then he remains stuck in the cave. To get unstuck he is drawn to solving little problems, like reading the news,

---

[59] Sahih Al-Bukhari 6846 - Vol. 8, Book 82, Hadith 829

watching TV, driving his car, doing physical exercise, watching a football game, playing basketball, and so forth. Any challenging activity that initially requires only 5 percent of his mind can assist him in forgetting his problems and becoming unstuck. Then the next day he can redirect his focus to his problem with greater success."

In accepting and respecting that this is the nature of men and that he needs time alone, two things happen. One, a woman no longer feels offended or takes her husband's need for space personally. And two, her husband feels accepted, which pulls him out of his distant state faster.

Grow × Learn × Live

While a man's needs are significantly less than a woman's, he too would benefit from consistent behaviours. Especially since we, women, tend to be inconsistent in our moods.

Consider implementing the following as a standard way of interacting, so that in these suggested subtle ways, you ensure you're always working on being a comfort to him:

- Be playful/flirt (at least once a day)
- Make yourself look good (at least once a week)
- Listen to him (at least once a day – 10 minutes)
- Serve him (at least once a day)
- Thank him (at least once a day)

Chapter 23 – Self Care

Love You and Be Loved

Two things that push couples over the edge are their inability to set time for themselves as a couple and set time for themselves as individuals (of course, everything in moderation).

To give all the warmth, affection, and good loving to your spouse, you must possess enough love within yourself first. You have to find peace and contentment within yourself (through the gifts that Allah has given you). Some like to call this "self-care" or "self-love" because you're taking a bit of time to be content with yourself. We need time to ourselves to feel whole and purposeful. An empty pitcher cannot fill anyone's cup!

Think of it like a mini "reset button" similar to the one we press on a router when the Wi-Fi goes down. Press the reset button, and you'll be able to keep serving. Allow all that junk to pile up, and you'd be constantly disconnecting from those you love the most!

Taking care of your emotional self is imperative in creating a harmonious marriage. Taking some time, even if it's 15 minutes a day or an hour every week, to do something that makes you excited will do wonders for your own emotional state. It can be as simple as reading a book, listening to a lecture, doing extra dhikr, or even getting lost in a hobby. The point is to make it *your time* to do something that brings *you* joy without feeling guilty about it. Try not to make devices an option during this time as studies have shown that excessive smart phone use leads to negative psychological effects (depression, anxiety, and insomnia).

Each spouse should actively support the other in taking individual time to nurture their own soul. For each person, this will mean something different. Just remember, the idea isn't to forgo responsibilities and become reckless. It means that within your duties, with the support of each other, time and space are accommodated to do something you each enjoy individually (as long as it's halal, of course!) in a guilt-free, loving, constructive, togetherness-yet-not kind of way.

Troubleshooting Self-Care

Our spouse is not responsible for our happiness, peace, or contentment in life. Of course, they influence it and sometimes make it difficult for us to get to that point, but they are not responsible for it (nor are our children). If we place the burden on our spouse (or children) to keep us feeling loved or fulfilled, we're setting ourselves up for disappointment. No one is created to do that. We are all created to worship Allah, which, in doing so, acts as a support for others and promotes loving, positive emotions.

If you're the type of person that feels you "need" (or very much want) to have your spouse near you every free moment they have, then you'll have to dig deeper within yourself to find what makes you happy. Keeping your spouse hostage to this type of unhealthy emotional neediness is overwhelming to your spouse and is a huge intimacy killer. It's suffocating for a partner to always be expected to be around. A spouse's role is not to continually keep reaffirming your actions, validating your feelings, etc. It's exhausting. You have to find fulfillment within yourself first, and then your spouse's role is to complement those feel-good vibes with their own vibes. Space is healthy, so you can keep adding fresh thoughts, discussions, and emotions to your relationship.

Marital Martyr

Serving people, doing good to people, taking care of loved ones, and making your husband or wife smile are all rewarding. However, if it's all you do, without giving yourself a second thought, thinking, "if they're happy, I'm happy," then you're lying to yourself. It's simply not true.

Neglecting yourself will not bring you happiness, nor will it give that to your spouse (or children). Here's the kicker though - your spouse is likely not even asking you to do that for them. Know, you can't fulfill your spouse and give them purpose in life, just as your spouse can't do that for you.

For some, they struggle with knowing what they like, need, want, or even enjoy. These individuals are typically suffering from what is known as the "martyr complex" or codependency issues. This means they continuously sacrifice their needs for the sake of others.

While being selfless is a noble quality, the codependent personality will do things for others because they feel guilty or ashamed of themselves (though that's not what they're telling themselves). They are continually offering themselves (unasked), and it is rarely reciprocated. Individuals become consumed by trying to "set things right" or keep "saving" their partner (or marriage) that they no longer recognize their own needs and wants. They deflect their emotions by affirming to themselves their good actions and the wholesome efforts they put forward. Unfortunately, that's rarely the truth behind the situation as they are merely trying to feel fulfilled, accepted, and validated without recognizing the same needs within themselves. Deep within, people with a martyr complex harbour disappointment and resentment for not having those needs met and their sacrifices acknowledged, the way they do to others. With that, they also feel shame in expressing such needs as they think they should be the one to "help," "be the bigger person," or feel "a Muslim must help another," etc. People that suffer from this do it by choice, as no one is actually asking them.

The person that codependents enable to neglect or pass-on their responsibilities is not someone that is actually "needy." This person doesn't constantly need help to rise above their situation(s), even if they appear pitiful in some way. Consequently, as codependents continue living for and through the other person, they lose themselves and can no longer function as an individual.

For a Muslim, codependent behaviours can easily be justified as being a good Muslim. While a believer serves and continues to give without wanting anything in return or reminding anyone of the favours they do, they must understand "good" needs to be balanced. Also, "giving" for Allah won't make anyone feel at a loss.

Conquering a codependent nature requires one to take a deep look within. They will have to acknowledge what they are running away from and the fears they are deflecting. They may discover that they do not feel they "deserve love" or are "not good enough to be loved" without constantly making themselves available. To that mentality, I say - you are enough. Allah created you with gifts, strengths, weaknesses, beauty, and faults, just like everyone else. Again, you are enough. You need no longer have to feel the need to go above and beyond to become worthy of being loved. You know better than most that no matter how much you give, you are still left wondering where things went wrong. Therefore, understand that it is your responsibility to learn to manifest your beautiful self through balance, confidence, and ultimately ensuring your needs are met; unapologetically.

Grow × Learn × Live

Think of what makes you feel happy (away from your partner) and write it down. Then decide with your spouse when a good time to do that would be. Encourage him/her to do the same.

Take time away from the daily grind to do something you like, even if it's reading a book. It will be mentally refreshing for the both of you!

Chapter 24 – Gratitude

Developing an Attitude of Gratitude

> "And [remember] when your Lord proclaimed, 'If you are grateful, I will surely increase you [in favour]; but if you deny, indeed, My punishment is severe.' " *(Quran 14:7)*

Is there comfort in complaining? I think to a certain degree, there's this idea that if we state our grievances, then they will go away - but they never do. If anything, they just become that much more draining as they take up precious brain space.

In Western society, general dialogue is surrounded around criticizing and complaining. It's toxic, yes, but it's almost natural in this environment. It's a plague that we cannot see, despite it causing so much destruction and turmoil in our lives. This disease of the heart, that affects our internal and external spiritual state, stems from ingratitude.

I honestly would not have considered myself as someone that's "ungrateful" because I felt I noticed the blessings in my life, but while seeing one good thing, I also found nine things that were not so good. Even if I did not express them outwardly, they still sat within.

The perpetual state of complaining: the house is small, the grass isn't green enough, the food is too spicy, the grapes have seeds, the air conditioner is too cold, the wife is controlling, the husband is lazy, the cat keeps shedding, the baby doesn't stop crying, etc. gives us nothing back in return except the feeling of "blah."

It never ends.

It has taken me some serious work to realize I have been missing out on a very critical and foundational piece in life - the manifestation of genuine gratitude.

The Prophet, peace and blessings be upon him, said in response to the question: "…O Messenger of Allah what kind of wealth should we acquire?" He said: "Let one of you acquire a thankful heart, a tongue that remembers Allah and a believing wife who will help him with regard to the Hereafter."[60]

Choose to Experience the Joys of Life, Not the Reverse

We can always make a choice to find flaws in our spouse. They are as human as we are, but in doing so, it will suck the joy out of our life. Taking the time to develop a heart of gratitude is one of the most beneficial practices you can do for your life and family.

Cultivating a grateful heart is a form of worship. It breeds peace and contentment, it increases the goodness in your life - both in this world and the hereafter, it causes one to become humble, and it saves us from becoming hardhearted. It's a real game changer!

Manifesting gratitude comes in different forms. It's not limited to only verbally acknowledging the good things you can see or feeling grateful when you get what you want. That's the first step. Thereafter it manifests into actions:

- **Good Deeds:** Giving to others, serving them with our time or knowledge without seeking any type of gain.
- **Dhikr/Remembering Allah:** Praising Allah (alhamdulilah) in all areas of our life.
- **Repentance:** When we acknowledge good done to us, we become humbled and overwhelmed by these favours. Gratitude enables us to find humility, and within humility, we can recognize our wrongs and seek to make them right.

The concept of acknowledging the favours done to us is known, even in Western psychology, to increase a person's mental and physical well-being. Unfortunately, sometimes people have a harder time developing gratitude because there are other characteristics within themselves that they first need to shed away. Studies have found that traits which act as barriers towards attaining gratitude include: envy, materialism, narcissism, and cynicism. Of course, there's no better start towards developing gratitude than by asking Allah to bestow this quality upon us, the way Prophet Sulaiman, peace be upon him, had asked.

---

[60] Sunan Ibn Majah Vol. 3, Book 9, Hadith 1856

"My Lord enable me to be grateful for Your favour which You have bestowed upon me and upon my parents and to work righteousness of which You will approve and make righteous for me my offspring. Indeed, I have repented to You, and indeed, I am of the Muslims." *(Quran 46:15)*

    In marriage, where you see the same person day-in and day-out, it's easy to take what they do for granted. It's easy to forget that your wife doesn't get excited about cleaning the bathroom, cooking in the kitchen for some hours or dealing with tantrums, but she does those things anyway. It's easy to forget that your husband hates the fact that he has to get up early every day to a gruelling commute, struggle to make it on time for salah or make wudhu in a public restroom, has to deal with people that don't share the same values as him, but he does those things anyway. Yes, both partners are fulfilling their duties, but a healthy marriage recognizes these sacrifices by giving thanks and not dismissing them with an attitude of entitlement ("well, it's my right").
    After making dua'a, the effort required to develop gratitude is to thank those around you daily, for all the good they do in which you benefit from. Thanking the people for their graciousness upon you is an act of worship.

The Prophet, peace and blessings be upon him, gave us this very strong instruction, because he repeated it twice, he said: "Whoever is not grateful to the people, he is not grateful to Allah."[61]

Asma, may Allah be pleased with her, reported: The Messenger of Allah, peace and blessings be upon him, passed by a group of women in the mosque one day. The Prophet, peace and blessings be upon him, waved with his hand to greet them with peace and he said, "Beware of ingratitude to those who bless you. Beware of ingratitude to those who bless you." One of the women said, "O Messenger of Allah, I seek refuge in Allah, O Prophet of Allah, from being ungrateful to Allah." The Prophet, peace and blessings be upon him, said, "Rather, one of you will be widowed for a long time throughout her middle years, then Allah provides her with a husband and he

---

[61] Jami Al-Tirmidhi 1954 - Vol. 4, Book 1, Hadith 1954

benefits her with a child, the joy of her life. Then, she gets very angry and she swears by Allah, saying: I never had one good moment with you! That is ingratitude to the blessings of Allah. That is ingratitude to those who bless her."[62]

Ali bin Abi Talib, may Allah be pleased with him, said: "Blessings arrive with gratitude (to Allah), and gratitude is connected with more (blessings), and the two are tied together: more blessings from Allah will never stop unless gratitude from the servant stops." [63]

Grow × Learn × Live

It takes conscious efforts and practice to develop good habits. Every day, at least once a day, acknowledge the good your spouse does for you. To say "thank you" for what you ask is common courtesy. Saying thank you and the du'aa of "jazakaAllah khayran" - may Allah reward you with the best - to your spouse for doing things that you appreciate but didn't directly ask for (i.e., cooking, fixing the car, attending to children, bringing home groceries, etc.) is empowering to your spouse and humbling for you. Try to do this daily, without fail.

---

[62] Musnad Aḥmad 27042
[63] Ibn Abi Al-Dunya, Al-Shukr - Article 18

Chapter 25 – Putting Polygyny into Perspective

"If you fear that you will not do justice to the orphans, then, marry the women you like, in twos, in threes and in fours. But, if you fear that you will not maintain equity, then (keep to) one woman, or bondwomen you own. It will be closer to abstaining from injustice." *(Quran 4:3)*

The Secular Perspective

Polygyny is defined as when a man marries more than one wife. Secular governments prohibit the practice of polygyny citing, "Under international human rights law, there is a growing consensus that polygyny violates women's rights to be free from all forms of discrimination."

As well,

> "Polygamous marriage contravenes a woman's right to equality with men, and can have such serious emotional and financial consequences for her and her dependents that such marriages ought to be discouraged and prohibited."[64]

The above-mentioned holds true if polygyny is practiced without any parameters or rules. However, within Islamic law, absolute equal rights have been given to women, so much so that a man is accountable before Allah in ensuring this equality is granted. There is no greater accountability than that!

So for us as believers who have chosen to submit to Allah, we are not to accept the belief that polygyny lacks equality. How can that be true if the Most Just has allowed for it and regulated the practice under a set of defined conditions? The laws of the land are one thing but accepting the belief that it is not "equitable," or worse, not "right," is a total violation of our submission to Allah's laws.

Allah, in His wisdom, would not allow for women to be treated without equality. Polygyny, in fact, provides every right be given to a

---

[64] CEDAW noted in its Genera Recommendation no.21 on Equality in Marriage and Family Relations

woman, ensuring that her dignity and the welfare of the children she bears are preserved.

Interestingly enough, the debate of polygyny in some communities has chosen to overlook the social crisis in which open sexual practices are accepted as "a freedom of one's right"; as long as it's not imposed under any set of religious-based rulings or laws. Thus, couples can mutually agree to an "open marriage," allowing free access to any sexual partner they choose without any legal repercussions.

Secular law permits the conception of children even with no knowledge of their biological father. The instability it causes these children is still evident late into their adulthood. The knowledge and lineage of one's biological parents is a right Islam has given a child, and Western governing laws that claim to advocate human rights violate the rights of children by allowing this to happen. They support the freedom to do with oneself as we choose. Still, if it's in the context of securing a woman's dignity, children's identities, and familial stability, then it is deemed as inequitable.

In Islam, a woman retains all her wealth unless she so chooses to give it away. This forces men to be fully accountable for providing for the homes under their care. However, in an overview of secular law, the husband is entitled to half of his wife's wealth. He can decide to use her and abuse her in marriage, file for divorce and uphold "equal rights" to take fifty percent of all she has earned. Through secular laws, she has equal responsibility and must pay up, but Islamically she has the right to keep every penny she earns, an Islamic law that Muslims don't hesitate to uphold when it's in their best interest. So, why do some Muslims argue strict adherence to the laws of the land when they seem to be in their favour, yet oppose them when these laws are in-line with their nafs (desires)?

Another point in the debate of gender equality is: "Should a man hit a woman back if she hits him?" Most people still say, "No, you can never hit a woman," but if they are equal and he has the right to equality regardless of gender, wouldn't it be "just" to reciprocate the same actions?

Picking and choosing does not determine what's "right" and "wrong." It is only for Allah to determine the criterion of right and wrong, with which is the ultimate truth, fairness, and wisdom.

The Hypocrisy in Polygyny

Many Muslims advocating for or against polygyny fall prey to the idea that we can freely choose Islamic laws that suit our "needs" and desires without considering them as a complete system. Unfortunately, through excessiveness, the very idea of polygyny has been corrupted, regardless of which side one is on.

Typically, women will reject polygyny citing a lack of fairness. While men will embark on it without either having the means to equally provide financially and/or physically while also infringing on the rights of their present wife. There's nothing Islamic about this.

When polygyny is approached with the utmost seriousness and with a consciousness of Allah, only then will it become a means of ease for everyone involved, by Allah's grace and permission.

Some women say they would rather their husband commit zina (fornication) than take another wife. This type of understanding is so dangerous for a believer!

One: She is putting herself above the laws of Allah - the King of Kings! Two: Simply by saying it, she takes sin lightly. Three: She doesn't actually care about her husband. Her main concern is herself, whether it's in what other people think of her or it's in how she feels (possibly even both). Faith cannot flourish when mixed with the acceptance of explicitly haram (forbidden) acts. Regardless of what one's ego accepts, it will never amount to goodness.

The Mousetrap Men Step In

Some men say that they can marry whoever they want, and they don't have to tell their wife. True, there is no obligation to inform one's wife, but there is also no wisdom in hiding it from her, especially if he is taking it as a serious matter of rights and responsibilities. The trap men find themselves in tends to present polygyny only as a right of his and not a responsibility on him. He gets caught when he fails to see polygyny in its entirety, as both a right and also an increase in responsibilities.

When a man chooses to become secretive with the cowardly approach of "protecting" his first wife's emotions, he turns a potentially positive, blessed undertaking (even though it's hard) into something ugly.

One: He will succumb to lying to cover the fact that he is with his other wife or with regards to finances especially so if she contributes to the household expenses. Two: Marriage in Islam should be open and made known to the people, therefore by hiding, he fails to do this. Three: The worst of all, he fears his wife over what Allah has made permissible (assuming he meets the imposed conditions).

Men believe that they are hiding polygyny to "protect" their already established marriage, but this explanation simply makes him the fool. Lying directly kills trust, and trust is the foundation of any and every healthy, thriving relationship. The reality (his ego won't like it) is he hides the truth because he's afraid of what his wife would say or do (divorce). For some men, fear likely comes from the fact that he's not fulfilling her due rights entirely anyway, which gives her grounds to walk away. A good man, one that takes care of his wife's needs, is not going to be easy to part with – he knows that.

Polygyny Doesn't Reflect A Woman's Value

Muslim women become staunch advocates against polygyny regardless of whether a man fulfills her full Islamic rights. She feels she has been "replaced" or fears judgement associated with the social stigma of polygyny suggesting something must be "wrong with her" in some way. Her jealousy, or rather insecurity, as well as fear of people's opinions have allowed her to transgress even her belief in the permissibility of plural marriage for a man.

As believers, this must change! There was nothing defective about the Prophet's wives, may Allah be pleased with them, nor were the wives he married "home wreckers." Yes, of course, we live in a different time which is why polygyny is very difficult to practice. Still, it should not be shunned or frowned upon, especially with the arrogance (and ignorance) that many Muslims don't hesitate in expressing.

Submitting to the Laws of Allah

Allah has perfected our religion, and it is He alone that created us! It is His right alone to dictate what is fair and what isn't. We have no right to say other than what He has allowed, despite our insecurities, jealousy, or desires. We can see from women that wholeheartedly submit to polygyny and with husbands that do not waiver in fulfilling the rights upon them (financial stability and emotional security through equal nights) that the family dynamics are very beautiful. The women form a friendship that offers them an emotional support that only a sister can give. We are not accustomed to this in Western societies since there is a level of ownership involved (mentioned in earlier chapters) that prevents women from benefiting from this blessing of a co-wife or "sister wife."

Polygyny Works When Your Established Marriage Is Healthy

A sexual relationship is the defining difference between a marriage and any other relationships, which is what makes polygyny so difficult for many women to accept but easy for men to. However, the pleasure and constancy we all seek will only come when we exert the necessary efforts to create this emotional stability. For a man, this effort would require a little less of his needs and a little more of hers. For a woman, this would require more of his needs and less of her insecurities. Together, balance can be sought, even as you go forth and introduce someone new within your family dynamics.

Polygyny cannot be sufficiently sustained when the current established marriage is not a secure, healthy marriage. If a man embarks on taking a second wife because he's trying to avoid dealing with the issues in his present marriage, he'll quickly find that he now has two problems. No matter how many wives a man has, it requires him to make an effort in establishing a harmonious marriage, similar to what is outlined in this book (and many others) to be the comfort he seeks.

No one can know your intention except you. As believers, men have to understand that the journey starts within themselves in seeking a second wife. How? By truly fearing Allah in his affairs and considering everyone and everything that his decision will affect, not just the intensity in seeking to "control" his desires.

The Secret to Polygyny

For polygyny to flourish with blessings, there needs to be a fundamental mindset. With this at the forefront of everyone's mind, Insha'Allah, each relationship will be beautiful in its own unique way, even if it is not "ideal."

The Messenger of Allah, peace and blessings be upon him, said, "None of you will believe until you love for your brother what you love for yourself."[65]

For the Brothers

Brothers, Be Careful - Know the Conditions First!

There is no doubt that polygyny is permitted in Islamic law, and it is a means of protection against many evils. However, this topic requires a level of maturity when discussing it. Polygyny is very emotionally driven and can cause both men and women to reject the laws of Allah – this holds equally true for those who are for or against polygyny.

Of course, Islam in its perfection has put conditions which a man must meet prior to marriage and even before "looking." Polygyny is not a loophole for men to deal with non-mahram women in the name of "marriage," when they don't even possess the means to fulfill their current responsibilities. Playing with Allah's laws and making a mockery of religion will only come back to bite you in the hereafter (may Allah protect us all, ameen).

The responsibilities a man must meet entail that he has the financial means to care for all households in perfect equality, based on the same standard of living each wife is used to. If he chooses to marry without meeting these conditions, he has essentially rejected the laws that make polygyny permissible. Therefore, embarking on polygyny doesn't "safeguard" him. It takes him away from Allah

---

[65] Jami Al-Tirmidhi - Vol. 4, Book 11, Hadith 2515

rather than bringing him closer, if he cannot fulfill the conditions on him first. He also has to maintain strict equality between homes, including where he spends his nights and what he gives. If he does not do this, then again, he is transgressing the rights he owes to others, thus making him sinful. A man cannot delude himself into thinking he's being righteous by taking a second wife, and all the while neglect fundamental characteristics of a believer (i.e., fulfilling rights of others).

A question that men like to pose is, *"What if a woman agrees to give up her rights since she's living independently anyway?"*

Scholars advise women against doing this. It places women at a disadvantage and ceases to be balanced, as Allah has made it. It forces a woman to continually be the breadwinner even though she has a husband whose greatest service to her is maintaining and protecting her from having to deal with that.

Well, what if she likes it? A hobby is different than a need or requirement. Also, it allows men to go beyond their means which can translate into greed and irresponsibility. While it's not impossible, it takes a special and rare man not to abuse this set of circumstances. Nonetheless, it is not advisable for women to enter into polygyny under these circumstances.

Unfortunately, as men occupy their time pursuing women with the "intent of marriage," they neglect the woman they already have. This is almost always going to cause intense marital discord nearing the point of divorce, if not leading to divorce itself. It's nothing but drama.

In every single relationship, each partner enters it with their own set of triggers, insecurities, issues, and traits that you may love or hate. Every marriage takes work to build the love and tenderness described as a happy marriage, so don't assume "the grass is greener on the other side."

It's Not Your Job to Convince Her, It's Your Job to Honour Her

I'm going to say it as it is, even if many women might not like it - a man does not need his wife's "permission" or approval before he takes another wife. The argument is, if she "agrees" then things will be a lot smoother – maybe or maybe not! A man has already been granted permission by our Master – how absurd to think that a wife's opinion will supersede what has already been stated by Allah and practiced by His Messenger, peace and blessings upon him. It makes no sense, and any woman that expects that she has the right to "grant permission" needs to take a second look at that!

With that being said, there is great wisdom, blessings, and overall goodness for the entire marriage if this desire of taking another wife is made clearly known.

Let's be real. The majority of women will not be ecstatic and jumping with joy about having a co-wife. Of course not. There are so many unknowns! Plus, nothing triggers a woman more than the threat of instability. This is normal, to be expected, and appreciated because it shows her love and attachment. It's not to be taken offensively, so learn to appreciate the nature of women. After all, her loyalty is one of the finest qualities to a man, even if it adds a few bumps along the way.

A man that is serious about bringing another wife into his family dynamics will also be man enough (yes, man enough) to be honest and act with integrity. His wife may not be happy, may use emotional blackmail, may give him the silent treatment, may become aggressive, may even threaten to divorce; it's expected. She's triggered! Lying, however, will destroy the good you do have in your marriage. It will destroy your present relationship, and for what? The allure of another wife, who may or may not love you, care for you, want the best for you, as the wife you may already have?

So, then what? How do you go about doing this?

Understand an angry, upset, sad wife reacts this way because she fears losing you. Losing your love, your protection, her easy access to you, her time with you, her self-confidence, pride in feeling she has a man who 'only' loves her, etc. Again, it's her nature. Your job is to secure all those emotions – not by convincing her about how another woman is going to give her emotional support or be her friend, or… blah, blah, blah, but rather by showing empathy to her and her emotions. Empathy doesn't mean you won't take a second wife, but it also doesn't allow blaming her for feeling what she feels. Rather, empathy shows you truly understand and appreciate her emotional connection to you.

I strongly suggest that if your wife gets deeply emotional about polygyny, you don't deal with the inevitable awkwardness by bringing religion into the discussion. Resist "reminding," lecturing, or stating your rights. While it's all true, by doing this, you will prove that you fail to see why she feels what she feels. Her feelings aren't religiously based. They're her own lowly desires versus your lowly desires. In that time, she is being tested in her faith, so don't throw it at her as there is no wisdom in it. Make the discussion about yourself: your dreams, your desires, etc. Not religion and definitely not how your actions are for her sake.

Go back to your relationship and solidify her needs. Make her worth apparent to both of you and make her confident in your commitment to her. She still won't likely be jumping for joy, but she'll have the support she needs to overcome her insecurities and most importantly the evils of people and Shaytaan. It's a battle she faces, and you should try to be sympathetic to that struggle. Deal with her in kindness, honesty, integrity, and fear Allah in your method of pursuing another wife.

It's None of Her Business

Wives that "come around" to the idea and seem accepting of it may also want to be involved in the "picking wife" process. It's really just a way for her to feel in control of her circumstances and not feel left out or abandoned. Don't allow this.

The relationship between you and your wives should always remain separate. What you think of each other, the complaints, joys, etc. should be in two different compartments. Don't involve your wife in picking who you marry because she then is involved in your relationship from the get-go. While she may seem "strong" and feel she can handle it, Shaytaan will use everything he knows to attack her. It is beyond the nature of a woman, so if you love her, don't let her take on that burden.

Nonetheless, when you do decide to start looking (likely online), tell her. Inform her how you do it (if she wants to know) and tell her you aren't going to keep secrets from her.

It looks something like this: "Baby *(insert word of endearment)*, as I've mentioned to you before, I want to start looking for another wife, and even if you don't understand, know that it doesn't take away from the love and admiration I have for you. I'm going to make a profile online *(insert method)* and see if something comes my way. I'm not trying to hurt you, even if you feel hurt. I'm telling you, so you know that I'm not going to destroy our marriage and the trust we have. I'm saying everything openly, so you trust I'm not keeping secrets from you."

…She still won't like it, but she'll respect it. That's what you want; to maintain that respect because when all is said and done, she'll have your integrity and honesty to fall back on.

She will have questions about finances and your ability to take care of two homes. It's a valid concern which you should be more worried about than she is. If you resolve with "Allah provides," while it's true, you're merely playing games. Of course, Allah provides, but we're required to make an effort. Two wives are not a necessity, so be real about involving another in your affairs. If you aren't ready, don't be greedy and go looking for someone beyond your capacity.

When Looking for Another Wife

Know what you want! Keep your standards clear and don't get sucked into the hype. Another wife is real, and while it has its perks, it's serious business. Don't get played by falling into the trap of being on the desperate side of things - you aren't. You already have a wife!

When interviewing another woman to be part of your life and your family, do not, under any circumstances (even if you're mad at your wife), insult your wife, belittle her, complain about her, or say anything negative about her. When the woman in question inevitably asks, "Why are you looking for a second wife?" - do not talk about your present wife. Say something general, "I feel like there's good in it, and I can handle it," etc.

When she asks, "What about your wife?" Again, respond by protecting your wife's honour (even if you two are upset with each other): "She's a good woman and I'm blessed to have her. Of course, it's difficult for her, but we respect each other, and she knows how committed I am to her."

That last answer will make or break this interview.

If the woman you're talking to can't handle the respect you have for your current wife, she's not going to want to support that relationship. She lacks the confidence, security, and knowledge to do so. Some women enter into polygyny convinced by him that he's "stuck in the marriage," she'll be the replacement, and that, in some way, he doesn't care about his wife. It's not nice, and it's the wrong intention when trying to create a positive family dynamic.

If you get the slightest whiff of those sentiments, run! It takes time to get a good one, so don't despair. After all, you aren't trying to ruin your current marriage, are you?

Remember to keep making dua'a and ask Allah to give you the ability, guidance, means and to make everyone a coolness and comfort to each other.

After that, fear Allah. You aren't married yet, don't talk to each other unnecessarily or unaccompanied; also, don't disrespect your wife either by answering texts and e-mails from a non-mahram woman. Involve a trusted third party (her wali/guardian, etc.) to protect yourself because Shaytaan will be in your mix looking to corrupt any goodness you're trying to achieve.

When You've Found Her

It's expected that it'll take some time to find a woman suitable and accepting of the conditions that will instantly be placed within your next marriage. Insha'Allah, when it happens, and you've done your due diligence, let your wife know. Lovingly tell her (don't overdo it with flowers and material things even if it's her love language, it comes with ulterior motives). Sit her down, "Babe, remember I told you I don't want to keep secrets from you and that I would let you know what I was doing? Well, someone has come along who I believe respects our relationship and is God-fearing. I have done istikhara and feel I want to marry her. I've dealt with her wali and set the nikkah for ___."

Her heart will drop. She may be silent. She may cry. She may lash out. She may be confused. She will start to grieve the loss of her marriage that she has come to know and love, so it is up to you to continue loving, praising, and securing the relationship. Even if she's mad, do not turn your back on her emotional needs. Perhaps she won't talk. Perhaps she won't even look at you. Perhaps in the night you'll hear her sobbing. Hold her hand, stroke her hair, and be there in the way you've always shown up in your marriage. BE THERE, patiently. It's hard, and through no fault of your own. This is just the way things are, and you have to be realistic about it.

Perhaps the issue of delaying things or compromising will come up. You, too, will be torn. You'll feel guilty and possibly feel "bad," but you aren't. It's not wrong to desire another wife. It's wrong if you can't or aren't caring for those that you take as your "flock." If you've maintained the rights of everyone involved, then know you are good. Don't allow your wife's emotions to trigger your state. You'll only bring that into your new relationship or cause unnecessary drama. Let her grieve. It's okay. You didn't betray her. You were honest and forthcoming, be proud of yourself for that!

When All Is Said and Done

Men like to think that if their wives are friends, then their relationship is successful. It's not true. You have to resist the urge to control both wives' relationship even if they try to involve you in it. Don't get involved. They are grown women. If they want to form a relationship, they will. They may even both want to meet before the marriage takes place, and that's fair to ask (but you shouldn't be there).

Despite your deepest desire for everyone to be "happy" and get along well, it is for your wives to decide how much they want to get involved with each other, so don't push it. If you push it, it may backfire. Leave it to its natural progression.

It's up to you to make your schedule clear and fair to both wives. As routine sets in and they see your maturity and kindness, they too will settle.

Be careful not to shun either of your wives in trying to make others comfortable. If you are the type of man concerned about how others perceive you and their judgements, you might want to reconsider polygyny altogether. Polygyny makes many people uncomfortable, and that includes Muslims. However, just because others are unaccepting, it doesn't give you the right to dismiss, hide, or pretend that you don't have another wife to appease them. Otherwise, to the wife you choose to treat this way, it will be extremely hurtful, unjust, and cause mistrust between you. If you don't fully accept polygyny as a sound, justified practice, then don't do it!

It'll be Hard for You Too!

This is often not spoken about, but I've heard it being said. Men go through a lot when they take another wife. Apart from all the emotions involved and the opinions of others, there are also their own feelings. Another wife isn't instant chemistry. She's a stranger, and it may feel weird. Setting up another home, going there, being away from your children, and the wife you're used to sleeping next to every night - it's tough and tiring, but realistically, this is to be expected.

Give yourself time to settle in even if you're feeling awkward and uncomfortable. Try and keep yourself grounded in your emotions and neutral to whatever is pulling at you (expect a lot of pulling!).

If you aren't the type of man that enjoys the company of family and children, then you might want to re-consider polygyny all together. Your attentiveness to your family and *active* presence is important for the mental and emotional well-being of the entire household. If you're struggling to show up for just one home, you won't successfully manage a second family. A man that enjoys his own space, and dreads "family time" or interacting with his family on their level, is not a good candidate for a multiple family lifestyle. We no longer live in a time where there is the support of a village to help raise our children. Rather, it's necessary that each partner continuously be active and present in nurturing their family.

Expect that you will be stressed out, so do not, under any circumstances mention divorce to either wife. You will not be in the right state of mind to make such a drastic decision until things become routine and you're more comfortable with how everything is working. Divorce is not the first option (ever), so don't mention it, even if you feel it. Mentioning it will create long-term instability, even after your stresses have subsided. So, be very careful to not allow

Shaytaan the joy of whispering with the threat of divorce within your relationship, it's ugly and the instability (a woman's primary need being stability) will linger.

Typically, within a year of consistency, things will settle into place, Insha'Allah. You'll have to work on building a whole new relationship: trust, triggers, children, finances, etc. while re-establishing your other one. It's all work. With good intentions though, Insha'Allah, it'll be worth it - in this world and the Hereafter!

To My Sisters

Sisters, It's Okay...

A Muslim woman must have a good opinion of her Creator, despite the emotional insecurity polygyny might trigger. Truth be told, the insecurity is already there, but this topic is simply an avenue for it to manifest itself.

Feminism has penetrated the minds of women beyond trying to establish fairness. In the name of equality, they have now forced women to work the same as men, despite the fact that a woman carries a child and a man does not. There is a growing aversion among non-Muslim women in the Western world to leave their newborn children and go back to work. The fitra (natural disposition) of women is to want to be with their children and raise them. This contemporary version of independence is breaking the backs of women and robbing them of the feministic joys awarded through their inherent inclinations.

As Muslim women, we must be careful that we do not allow a false sense of "love" or ownership to take us away from our Creator. We submit to Him even if there's a difficult situation within ourselves and opposing Allah's laws are validated through social indoctrination. The reality is that women who accept polygyny wholeheartedly, under the conditions and rights that they are given, have more time to themselves, more support, and fewer worries.

The "liberated," modern woman desperately craves her husband to profess his undying love and that he has no desire for any woman ever - not true, even under the best of circumstances! You would be a foolish woman to think a man only desires you; it defies his fitra (natural disposition). This is why if you look at social experiments where they ask random, straight men: "Can men and women can just be friends?" all of them said "no." Yet, when they asked women, most of them said "yes."

When we take it upon ourselves to use our lowly desires (which include insecurities and egos) as our guiding light, we no longer live a balanced life. Islam is perfection, without a shadow of a doubt. Allah set laws and standards with full knowledge of His creation. It is only our arrogance and the ways of Shaytaan that push us to try to debate what Allah has set as law, under the conditions He has appointed. Who are any of us to argue that?

Yes, you're right. We should follow the law of the land, but that does not give us the right to "become the law" and oppose what Islamic law allows, especially within our hearts. A man can't even be legally married to more than one wife according to Western law, as it is not recognized. According to Western law, another woman would be considered his mistress (who has absolutely no legal rights). Under the freedom of having an "open marriage," society readily accepts immorality. "Side chicks" are now understood as a social norm, both hidden and hated. It is merely semantics designed to remove the consciousness of God and to keep taxes in order.

Betrayal is one of the most difficult emotional states to overcome because it breaks a person. To accept polygyny is to be free of this! You cannot control people's hearts, and to reject even the concept of polygyny is trying to control something you have no control over. Just because you said "no," it doesn't mean he'll have more love for you; in fact, it will likely lead to the reverse of that.

A point to always remember about polygyny, first and foremost, is to accept it within your heart as a law that Allah has permitted. This is imaan (faith), and it will save us from a lot of regrets, Insha'Allah.

As for what your husband does, including if he is wronging you, know he is answerable to Allah for it. While it's not that you'd want harm for your husband due to his negligence, and of course, it would be great if you forgive him, your husband doesn't have "free rein" to do what he wants.

No One Can Replace You

Also know, without a doubt (or arrogance), that no one can be you. No one!

Islamically speaking, we are only to compare ourselves with each other in regard to religion. Thus, we can aspire to be better, but who you are in your core is unique to you. A co-wife will have her own faults and her own strengths, just as you do. She is neither better than you, nor are you better than her. You should know that no matter what, you are uniquely you, and no one can replace that. Don't for a second think that your husband will "forget you." Why choose to think so lowly of yourself, as if you are easily forgettable? You are not! Not age, not looks, not money, not intelligence, nothing will remove your worth except lousy character. Allah has blessed us all with the gift of our individual personality, and to deny it, even in attempts to be humble, is to be ungrateful.

Be proud of who you are. Acknowledge your shortcomings but don't turn yourself into something less or more than who you are. You will never find pleasure in it.

What is meant for you, no one can take away, even if they try, and it doesn't only apply to monetary gains. Also, what is not meant for you, you will never get, no matter how loud you kick and scream. Our duty before our Lord is to submit to His command and choose good. That's the only control we have actually been given. Work within that and you'll find everything you've ever desired, Insha'Allah!

Is Divorce a Good Option?

Some women choose to divorce their husband if he takes another wife (regardless of the laws of the land). Some even do it if their rights are fulfilled lovingly, equally, and in their entirety. Ultimately, her pride has allowed her to suffer a loss in life. A good man is not an easy find. Those women that make their marriage conditional upon a monogamous relationship claim to accept polygyny but say it's not for them because they don't want to (or as some say "can't") share their husband. These sentiments beg the question: What does "sharing a husband" actually entail?

In this entire book, I've strongly advocated stripping down surface-level "convictions" and resolving to live within the truth, regardless of how painful it may be, because that's where ultimate success lies. The issue of polygyny is so heavily layered with emotional triggers because it threatens social, individual, and cultural narratives we hold within ourselves. If your husband is a good man, whom you are pleased to be married to but wish to divorce if he marries another wife because you "can't do it," then know you are caught in Shaytaan's trap.

Many women are not bothered about having their husband around every night, but she can't bear the thought of another woman around him. Some don't even mind if he's flirting outside the home, as long as she does not see it and he's not going to marry her.

The question remains: Why?

Why is a woman okay with so many haram acts but not with what is permissible? Polygyny poses two potential issues for the first wife: actual time and emotional connectedness.

> *If he is with another woman, that means he doesn't love me or can't love me.*
> *If he has another wife, he won't be here, and I won't have attention; he'll just love her.*
> *If he has another wife, when will I see him? How will we do things together? He won't be around much.*
> *If he takes another wife, I can't financially do what I want.*
> *I can't bear the thought of him sleeping with another woman.*
> *He's replaced me, and I'm not his number one priority anymore etc.*

All your thoughts are valid concerns, but unless you address them and know the truth, don't make divorce an option. Trust me when I tell you, divorce is not easy to deal with. Your life will never feel or be the same as what you knew. Also, many people will treat you differently because of it. A good man is hard to find; if he respects you, takes care of you, is a good father, is trying to be conscious of Allah, then at the very least try to understand him. Try to work through things. Ask questions - it's okay, but don't jump to divorce. At the very least, respect that your husband is trying to do good by you and is honestly telling you how he feels. He could do many other things, and you may never know. Be glad that he isn't being manipulative or bringing diseases into your home.

All of life is hard, so "choose your hard" - don't assume you'd be better off divorced. But possibly he might be, if you're placing an ultimatum on him counter to what Allah has already given him permission for.

Considering Being a "2nd Wife"?

There is a social stigma also regarding the "2nd wife" - or rather, "the other wife." Phrases like "homewrecker" and "husband stealer" get used even in the Muslim community. Surely you don't think that the wives of the Prophet, peace and blessings be upon him, should be described in such a lowly way, such as Aisha, may Allah be pleased with her, his "second/other wife"? Sure, it isn't the norm in today's society, but the laws of Allah are for all time. To think otherwise is to try to lower Allah – Lord of the heavens and the earth, and everything in between!

Expect that as a second wife, not everyone is going to like you simply because you agreed to marry a man that already had a wife. It's halal (permissible), and it is a sunnah of the Prophet, peace and blessings be upon him, – marriage and polygyny. Their issues are with them, not you. Society would excuse you if you had a boyfriend or if you committed adultery; they may even feel sorry for you. As a second wife though, they'll be filled with a lot of negativity, and make sure on some level that you know that. This even applies to your close family members. That's just how polygyny is within society these days, regardless of what country you're in. If you are deeply affected by how others perceive you, then don't do it.

When considering entering into polygyny, you'll have to become hyperaware of your own emotions as well as those which the man in question brings forth. The reason for this is that polygyny instinctively creates a dynamic of comparison, and if you allow yourself to enter into that, you'll be in an ugly place. Your husband will also be fighting with those emotions. Hence, your awareness will allow you to spot it and remove yourself from it. Polygyny requires that you are comfortable with yourself and are not looking for someone to validate your self-worth.

If the man you're considering for marriage speaks badly about his present wife and that's comforting to you, then know that you aren't any better. If you feel you can replace someone, then be sure someone else can replace you. If a man talks negatively about his wife, eventually, when he gets bored of you and the novelty wears off, he'll be doing the same about you with someone else. Don't allow your natural insecurities to accept that you are better in any way, shape, or form. You are unique and special in your own way, and she is too in her own way.

A woman's mindset going into a polygynous marriage needs to be very respectful of the man's current relationship. She should not only want good in it, but she should honour them by not saying anything that may harm their marriage.

It is very possible your co-wife will have a mindset opposite to this. That's okay. She's entitled to feel how she wants to, as well, she is going through her own grieving period. Your actions are not dictated by hers and you are not Islamically required to be friends. Simply show respect as you would with any other believer. If your co-wife is not reciprocating that same courtesy, it is on her and has nothing to do with you. Rest assured, people's behaviour towards you isn't actually about you, it's about them. May Allah make it easy for everyone, ameen.

Co-Wife Code

Having a co-wife or a sister-wife takes on a different dynamic altogether. Each is bound together through one mutual but highly influential component: their husband. While co-wives may have different interests and overall personalities, it does not mean they cannot always be respectful towards each other.

There is no condition on co-wives to form a friendship or be around one another, so there's no pressure if it's not something you feel comfortable or secure with. It is possible you both may simply not take to each other; some people "click" and some don't. If both women do get along and they choose to form a relationship, it's for the sake of their own selves. A husband can still be a good husband even if his wives aren't close.

Creating a friendship requires mutual desire and cooperation. It's unfair to "test" each other or always judge each other. There's no goodness in being "close" just so you can feed your insecurities, either by becoming jealous or by being condescending. If that's the condition of a "friendship," then don't do it. It will only push you into a dark space that can become toxic to your internal state.

If you both decide to unite as sisters, look out for each other, share, care, and show genuine concern, then know you have allowed yourself to bloom and experience the full blessing of polygyny.

Despite what each wife decides, there are some wife codes that, if adhered to, will create a sense of respect and be considered good conduct. For the sake of goodness, these codes allow for a bit of leeway in terms of rights and nights.

- Do not talk about your husband as a husband. Don't discuss issues that you have between yourselves. Don't discuss your intimate details, including any loving gestures he may have done for you, don't complain about him, etc. Your marriage details are off the table! Discussing it only opens the doors to Shaytaan.
- Do not complain to your husband about your co-wife. Perhaps express concerns but don't put him in a situation where he has to pick sides. Your relationship with each other is not his problem.
- Do not leave any "passion marks" on him. It may accidentally happen, but some women become petty in doing this, as expressed in polygyny forums. It's immature and disrespectful.
- Do not involve the children in any of your issues. They are innocent, so don't create a toxic environment for them. This includes when his children are at their stepmother's home. Good treatment is a must!
- Do not demand that you have your "night" if the other wife is in need. Perhaps she is pregnant and almost due, perhaps her child is sick, and she needs him, etc. Cooperation is a form of respect, and even if you aren't "friends," you should still want goodness for each other. It's likely both will experience these urgent needs at some point.

Grow × Learn × Live

If polygyny is a topic in your home, then two things have to happen:

Men – Do your homework! Look into a wife's rights under polygyny, the differences in polygyny, and the greater degree of responsibilities you will be required to carry. Know what is required of you before you get into anything with your desires leading the way and destruction of all the good you know tumbling behind you (*the dramatic imagery is necessary to establish the level of seriousness with which this topic should be addressed*).

Women – Find peace within yourself. Submit to Allah. Don't worry - it is not your husband that gives you peace, joy, and happiness. It is Allah that grants it through His will. So, if you want that for yourself, turn to Allah. He is near and knows your struggles.

Chapter 26 – Get Calm

Centring Your Soul

Have you noticed how many people consider themselves "sensitive" or say, "Maybe, I'm just sensitive" because they are frequently offended by the actions of others?

In today's world, the way a person parks can offend us. Things knock us out of a seemingly calm state so quickly that it is as if we were standing on one toe alone. While criticizing won't solve anything, it's crucial we acknowledge in ourselves how we respond and address the root of why we react the way we do. Believe it or not, there is a good reason why we do it, and it's not because we're "just sensitive."

Society is very demanding, especially in the West. There are hundreds of "to-dos" that feel necessary to have a good life, or to be a good parent, or to "be happy," etc. Yet, those almost "basic" things cause us to become stressed, depressed, snappy, anxious, and filled with negativity. The rat race of the dunya (this worldly life) is painful to the soul. It sucks us dry and spits us out. We lose control over our true wants, and it spills over, crossing the boundaries of what we know to be right and wrong. We become distracted by the many things pulling at our attention, lose control over our children, and fall into forms of extreme behaviour, including excessive eating, consumerism, and entertainment. We are offended easily because we are not at peace within, as there seems to be no time for that!

Know with certainty that our religion is perfection! That even the smallest things that we are commanded to do will direct our soul, body, and mind into a state of contentment and peace, or what most people simply refer to as "happiness."

If our daily prayers were done right, we'd find ourselves being centred within, but even that, we're caught trying to squeeze them in between meetings, school commitments, errands, activities, etc. Of course, we are still praying, but when in a rushed state, our prayers fail to produce the full effects they are meant to offer us.

We would benefit tremendously if we develop the habit of turning to Allah, pleading to Him for the ability to understand, for the strength to follow such teachings, and a way out from all our struggles. Without that, we'll never figure out what's wrong. Conscientious remembrance of Allah is a door to these realizations. It's glorifying and praising Him while being fully present. The quantity of worship is useless when we don't have quality attached to it (it's like dollar store products, they just keep breaking!).

Allah's Messenger, peace and blessings be upon him, said, "Verily, the hearts of all the sons of Adam are between the two fingers out of the fingers of the Compassionate Lord as one heart. He turns that to any (direction) He likes." Then Allah's Messenger, peace and blessing be upon him, said: "0 Allah, the Turner of the hearts, turn our hearts to Thine obedience."[66]

Our hearts need us to find a place of calm. We owe it to our soul to do that so that we can go through life with both feet planted. With that, we will be equipped with a softened heart necessary to give people the benefit of the doubt as is advised to us by the Prophet, peace and blessings be upon him. It is when we find this peace, we can take a step back and say, "It doesn't matter what people do, I'll keep trying to be a better me." (Insha'Allah)

> "Those who believe (in the Oneness of Allah - Islamic Monotheism) and whose hearts find rest in the remembrance of Allah. Verily, in the remembrance of Allah do hearts find rest." *(Quran 13:28)*

Peaceful Peace

A content soul and a peaceful life are within our grasp. The beautiful thing about it is that it doesn't require anyone or anything around us to be "right." We achieve this centring of the soul through du'aa (supplication) and dhikr (remembrance of Allah).

It's vital to our peace of mind that we make it a priority to take time out of our busy schedules and recite the praises of Allah, as well as ask for strength, peace, and guidance. Modern trends have latched onto yoga to offer people a sense of calm, but Islam in its perfection has already given us the perfect way:

---

[66] Sahih Muslim 2655 - Book 33, Hadith 6418

The Messenger of Allah, peace and blessings of Allah be upon him, said: "Whoever glorifies Allah (**says *Subhaan Allah***) thirty-three times immediately after each prayer, and praises Allah (**says *Al-hamdu Lillaah****)* thirty-three times, and magnifies Allah (says ***Allahu akbar***) thirty-three times, this makes ninety-nine, then to complete one hundred says ***Laa ilaaha ill-Allaah wahdahu laa shareeka lahu, lahul-mulk wa lahul-hamd wa huwa ala kulli shayin qadeer*** (There is no god except Allah alone, with no partner, His is the power and His is the praise, and He is able to do all things) his sins will be forgiven even if they are like the foam of the sea."[67]

In increasing the remembrance of Allah, we are cultivating a sense of awareness of Allah in our daily lives. Eventually, this leads to recognizing His majesty and authority over us. It humbles us, and it begins developing what is known as "taqwa" – a consciousness of Allah or, as it is sometimes translated, a "fear of Allah."

In this state, of heighted awareness of Allah, we fear transgressing the laws and obligations He puts upon us. We suck up our ego and overlook faults because we know we have many and hope that Allah will forgive ours. We have empathy and compassion because our heart has softened (i.e., humility) due to remembering Allah. We are also pro-active and aware of our words and actions, so we have better control over our raw emotions. We are not triggered as quickly because our purpose is higher than worldly pursuits. Our pursuit becomes our home in Jannah which we aren't willing to sabotage, especially for petty reasons.

Nothing can stop us from getting there except ourselves. Shaytaan has no control over us, none. He just calls (and annoys us like a whiny child), and we give in. Have patience and don't give in. Put him on mute with dhikr (remembrance of Allah).

"The Satan will say when the matter will have been decided, 'Allah promised you a truthful promise while I gave you a promise and did not fulfill it. I had no authority over you, except that I invited you and you accepted my call. So, do not blame me, but blame yourselves. Neither I can come to your help, nor can you come to

---

[67] Muslim - Book 2, Hadith 322

my help. I disown your associating me with Allah in the past. Surely, there is a painful punishment for the unjust.'" *(Quran 14:22)*

> ### Grow × Learn × Live
>
> Saying "alhamdulilah" – praise is due to Allah, is considered both du'aa and dhikr. Also, it develops a heart of gratitude. Start right now, at this very moment, and set your intention of coming closer to Allah and achieving the above-mentioned goodness, Insha'Allah.

Chapter 27 – Protection

Shaytaan is in Your Marriage

As stated in earlier chapters, the shayateen (army of Iblis) is actively trying to destroy marriages. This is especially so for those who seek to protect themselves from haram (forbidden acts), try to please Allah and work to develop a home that is founded on the teachings of Islam. After all, why go to great lengths to make someone go astray when they are already doing it themselves?

It would be foolish for us not to take the threat of the devil and his influence in our lives seriously:

> "O you who believe! Enter perfectly in Islam (by obeying all the rules and regulations of the Islamic religion) and follow not the footsteps of Shaitan (Satan). Verily! He is to you a plain enemy." (*Quran 2:208*)

If you've read this book in its entirety, then you've gathered I have been married a couple of times. I don't say it with pride, but my experience has allowed me to realize things that others may not be able to. The whisperings of Shaytaan are real, especially in marriage. I used to believe that they were my true thoughts, but in having to go through various experiences, I noticed the same thoughts kept emerging. It took me some time, but I eventually realized those were not actually my thoughts. It would be a crazy coincidence for the same views to hold true in such different circumstances. I understand how strange this might sound, but I am thoroughly convinced that waswasa (the whisperings of the devil) deeply affect marriages.

The point is that it's foolish to think that you are only two in your marriage and that there isn't something blowing thoughts of lies by fueling natural occurrences in a healthy marriage (taking those small arguments and turning them into reasons for divorce). Negative suggestions make it easy to stay stuck in the past, refuse to overlook faults, create "alternative facts," etc.

Rest assured, Allah will not leave us and has not left us. We have protection and safety against these hidden attacks that we think are from ourselves, but really they aren't.

I'm of the mindset that Muslims are pro-active. We don't just learn, we do. So, to conclude, I end with very special du'aas to help us on our journey, much in the same way as I began this book.

The Messenger of Allah, peace and blessings be upon him, said, "Whoever enters a residence and then says, 'I seek refuge in the perfect words of Allah from the evil of what He created,' nothing will harm him until he departs from that residence."[68]

The Messenger of Allah, peace and blessings be upon him, said (to Abdullah ibn Khubayb), "Speak". He replied, "What should I say?" The Prophet, peace and blessings be upon him, said, "Say: He is Allah, the One, (112:1) and the two chapters of refuge, al-Falaq and al-Nas, every evening and morning three times. They will be enough for you against everything."[69]

The Sincerity – Surah Al Ikhlas – *Quran 112*

بِسْمِ اللَّهِ الرَّحْمَنِ الرَّحِيمِ

Bismillah Ar-Rahman Ar-Raheem
In the name of Allah, The Most Gracious and The Most Merciful

قُلْ هُوَ اللَّهُ أَحَدٌ ﴿١﴾ اللَّهُ الصَّمَدُ ﴿٢﴾ لَمْ يَلِدْ وَلَمْ يُولَدْ ﴿٣﴾ وَلَمْ يَكُن لَّهُ كُفُوًا أَحَدٌ ﴿٤﴾

Qul huwa Allāhu ahadun. Allāhu al-ṣamadu. Lam yalid wa-lam yūlad. Wa-lam yakun lahu kufuwan ahadun.

Say, "He is Allah, [who is] One,
Allah, the Eternal Refuge.
He neither begets nor is born,
Nor is there to Him any equivalent."

---

[68] Ṣaḥīḥ Muslim 2708
[69] Sunan Al-Tirmidhi 3575

The Daybreak - Surah Al Falaq – *Quran 113*

بِسْمِ اللهِ الرَّحْمَنِ الرَّحِيمِ

Bismillah Ar-Rahman Ar-Raheem
In the name of Allah, The Most Gracious and The Most Merciful

قُلْ أَعُوذُ بِرَبِّ الْفَلَقِ ﴿١﴾ مِن شَرِّ مَا خَلَقَ ﴿٢﴾ وَمِن شَرِّ غَاسِقٍ إِذَا وَقَبَ ﴿٣﴾ وَمِن شَرِّ النَّفَّاثَاتِ فِي الْعُقَدِ ﴿٤﴾ وَمِن شَرِّ حَاسِدٍ إِذَا حَسَدَ ﴿٥﴾

Qul aʿūdhu bi-rabbi al-falaqi. Min sharri mā khalaqa. Wa-min sharri ghāsiqin idhā waqaba. Wa-min sharri al-naffāthāti fī al-ʿuqadi. Wa-min sharri ḥāsidin idhā ḥasada.

Say, "I seek refuge in the Lord of daybreak
From the evil of that which He created
And from the evil of darkness when it settles
And from the evil of the blowers in knots
And from the evil of an envier when he envies."

The Mankind – Surah Al Nas – *Quran 114*

بِسْمِ اللهِ الرَّحْمَنِ الرَّحِيمِ

Bismillah Ar-Rahman Ar-Raheem
In the name of Allah, The Most Gracious and The Most Merciful

قُلْ أَعُوذُ بِرَبِّ النَّاسِ ﴿١﴾ مَلِكِ النَّاسِ ﴿٢﴾ إِلَهِ النَّاسِ ﴿٣﴾ مِن شَرِّ الْوَسْوَاسِ الْخَنَّاسِ ﴿٤﴾ الَّذِي يُوَسْوِسُ فِي صُدُورِ النَّاسِ ﴿٥﴾ مِنَ الْجِنَّةِ وَالنَّاسِ ﴿٦﴾

Qul aʿūdhu bi-rabbi al-nāsi. Maliki al-nāsi. Ilāhi al-nāsi. Min sharri al-waswāsi al-khannāsi. al-Ladhī yuwaswisu fī ṣudūri al-nāsi. Min al-jinnati wa-al-nāsi.

Say, "I seek refuge in the Lord of mankind,
The Sovereign of mankind,
The God of mankind,
From the evil of the retreating whisperer –

Who whispers [evil] into the breasts of mankind –
From among the jinn and mankind."

رَّبِّ اَعُوْذُ بِكَ مِنْ هَمَزٰتِ الشَّيٰطِيْنِ. وَاَعُوْذُ بِكَ رَبِّ اَنْ يَّحْضُرُوْنِ.

Rabbi 'a`outhubika min hamazaatish-shayaateeni, wa 'a`outhu bika rabbi 'ay-yahdhuroon

"My Lord! I seek refuge with You from the whisperings (suggestions) of the Shayatin (devils). And I seek refuge with You, My Lord! Lest they may attend (or come near) me." *(Quran 23:97-98)*

Chapter 28 – Inspiration

Behind the Name '2 Seas' Muslim Marriage

> "And the two seas (kinds of water) are not alike, this fresh sweet, and pleasant to drink, and that saltish and bitter. And from them both you eat fresh tender meat (fish), and derive the ornaments that you wear. And you see the ships cleaving (the seawater as they sail through it), that you may seek of His bounty, and that you may give thanks." *(Quran 35:12)*

The inspiration behind the name '2 Seas' Muslim Marriage comes from surah Fatir (The Originator), verse twelve in the Quran.

I had come across this ayah when I opened the Quran looking for guidance and inspiration when trying to find a name. The first verse I read was the above-mentioned, and I felt that I needed to pay better attention to it.

When I first read this verse, my thought was that the wisdom I can take from it may be perhaps one spouse is sweet and the other bitter. But after much reflection, I realized something very profound. To me, in relation to what I sought guidance for, I learned that we could choose to be sweet or bitter (salty) in our marriage. We all go through both states within a marriage (expansion stage [sweet] and contraction stage [bitter]). While oftentimes in marriage we want to blame something or someone, this verse reminds me of self-accountability.

Also, it reminds me of how necessary and natural both states are. In both conditions, there is goodness. We can learn from the things that hurt in a marriage so as to push us to become better and adorn ourselves with good character. We, as humans, need freshwater to survive, and therefore the best state for us to be in is "fresh and sweet" and pleasant to be around which entails good character.

As well, it is with and through our spouses that we seek bounties and comfort - within that, we are blessed. It is a reminder to give thanks. Though we forget, when we learn to manifest gratitude in our marriage, it absolutely changes the way we see everything within it.

Developing true gratitude is a turning point in the way we perceive our lives, and it is key in achieving the goodness we seek within marriage. Allah knows best!

This book sets high standards for Muslim marriages, and while it appears unattainable, it isn't - if we keep striving, asking, and thinking good of Allah. It will take time, possibly even a lifetime. Truth be told, even if we manage a portion of what's in this book, we'll be on our way to something special. At the very least, it won't be bitter, Insha'Allah!

I leave you with a hadith that I believe should echo within us because it is only through our limitations that we perceive things to be unachievable, but for Allah, it is easy! Nothing happens without His permission, so think good thoughts and work hard – May Allah grant you success in both worlds – Ameen.

Allah's Messenger, peace and blessings be upon him, said, "Allah said, 'I am to my slave as he thinks of Me, (i.e., I am able to do for him what he thinks I can do for him)."[70]

I ask that Allah benefit those who read this, and He forgives me for all my shortcomings. May He protect the words within this book from relaying anything that displeases Him and goes against His perfect way - Ameen.

May Allah guide us all towards good. May He continuously put love and mercy in our marriages, bless our homes, our efforts, and give us the ability to do the work required to achieve peace and comfort in our marriages - Ameen.

الحمد لله ربّ العالمين

Al-hamdu lillahi rabbil 'alamin

---

[70] Sahih Al-Bukhari 7505 - Vol. 9, Book 93, Hadith 596

About the Author:

Shireen Patel is an author and a marriage coach for Muslim women. She has a lifelong obsession with "happily-ever-after" and it has been a journey she would have never imagined. Blessed to finally have that, she gratefully holds the badge of *"been there, done that!"* Through years of failure, success, passionate study, and much practice she found her calling in helping Muslim women transform their struggling marriages. Her superpower *(Masha'Allah)*? It's her ability to take surface level conflicts and pinpoint the core issue(s) to allow for healing and welcome change. Her platform 2SeasMuslimMarriage.com offers articles, courses, virtual group q/a's and 1-on-1 coaching (limited availability).

Made in the USA
Columbia, SC
14 October 2021